THE GREAT LAKES

An Environmental Atlas and Resource Book

Jointly produced by:

Environment Canada
Conservation and Protection, Ontario Region
Great Lakes Environment Program and
Water Planning and Management Branch
Toronto and Burlington, Ontario

United States Environmental Protection Agency
Great Lakes National Program Office
Chicago, Illinois

Brock University
Institute of Urban and Environmental Studies
St. Catharines, Ontario

Northwestern University
Center for Urban Affairs and Policy Research
Evanston, Illinois

1987

CONTRIBUTORS

ACKNOWLEDGEMENTS

Principal Authors

Lee Botts
Center for Urban Affairs
and Policy Research
Northwestern University
Evanston, Illinois

Bruce Krushelnicki
Institute of Urban
and Environmental Studies,
Brock University
St. Catharines, Ontario

U.S./Canada Steering Committee

Daryl Cowell
Conservation and Protection, Ontario Region
Great Lakes Environment Program
Environment Canada
Toronto, Ontario

Tom Clarke
Water Planning and Mangement Branch
Inland Waters/Lands Directorate
Environment Canada
Burlington, Ontario

Kent Fuller
Great Lakes National Program Office
United States
Environmental Protection Agency
Chicago, Illinois

Brock University Cartography Group

Alun Hughes, Cartographic Editor
Department of Geography

Cartographers:
Loris Gasparotto
Department of Geography
Peter Brown
Department of Geological Sciences

Editorial Assistants:
Alan Wilson
Ian Duquemin

Graphics

Luanne Lewandowski
Chicago, Illinois

The following people and agencies have provided valued assistance to this project by providing information, reviewing or contributing to text, or by making helpful comments. While their contributions are here acknowledged, the responsibility for errors or omissions rests with the principal authors, the cartographic editor and the U.S./Canada steering committee.

Production of the atlas was supported in part by grants from the Joyce Foundation and the Donner Foundation of the United States.

The contents were reviewed by some of the participants in the 1982-1985 Interuniversity Great Lakes Seminar sponsored by the Institute for Environmental Studies, University of Toronto, and the Center for Urban Affairs and Policy research, Northwestern University.

J.M. Anderson, Department of Geography, Concordia University, Montreal, Quebec

A.G. Ballert, Great Lakes Commission Ann Arbor, Michigan

A. Beeton, Great Lakes Environmental Research Laboratory, NOAA, Ann Arbor, Michigan

R. Beltram, U.S. Environmental Protection Agency, Great Lakes national Program Office, Chicago, Illinois

F. Berkes, Institute of Urban and Environmental Studies Brock University, St. Catharines, Ontario

M. Brooksbank, Regional Director General's Office, Conservation and Protection, Ontario Region, Environment Canada

V. Cairns, Canadian Department of Fisheries and Oceans, Burlinton, Ontario

D. Coleman, Inland Waters and Lands Directorate, Environment Canada, Burlington, Ontario

M. Dickman, Department of Biological Sciences Brock University St. Catharines, Ontario

G. Francis, Department of Environment and Resource Studies, University of Waterloo, Waterloo, Ontario

A. Hamilton, International Joint Commission, Ottawa, Ontario

C.E. Hendendorf, Ohio Sea Grant, Put-In Bay, Ohio

S. Leppard, Land Use Research Associates, Toronto, Ontario

J. Lloydd, CCIW, Burlington, Ontario

J. Middleton, Institute of Urban and Environmental Studies Brock University, St. Catharines, Ontario

G.K. Rodgers, National Water Research Institute, Environment Canada, Burlington, Ontario

R.M. Shipley, Welland Canals Preservation Association, St. Catharines, Ontario

W. Sonzogni, Wisconsin State Laboratory of Hygiene, University of Wisconsin, Madison, Wisconsin

J.R. Vallentyne, Canadian Department of Fisheries and Oceans, Burlington, Ontario

CONTENTS

CONTENTS (continued)

MAPS

FIGURES

GREAT LAKES FACTSHEETS

MESSAGE FROM THE CANADIAN MINISTER AND THE UNITED STATES ADMINISTRATOR FOR THE GREAT LAKES: AN ENVIRONMENTAL ATLAS AND RESOURCE BOOK

This atlas has been sponsored by the Canadian and American governments for citizens of the Great Lakes Basin. In undertaking this work, a primary goal was to provide an understanding of the "ecosystem approach". This approach forbids us to look at any element in the basin, including humans, in isolation. Rather, we see clearly the relationship we have to other parts of the system and the chain effect our actions have on all others.

The atlas is an essential tool in helping us understand the fragile and complex ecosystem of the Great Lakes. The authors have examined natural factors, such as geology, lake levels, and wetland habitats, to provide a basis from which we can begin to assess impacts on the system. We trace the earliest settlers who began to cut the trees, farm the land, and whose descendants eventually spawned the massive urban and industrial growth we know today. These developments went hand in hand with the eutrophication problems caused by excessive amounts of phosphorus. Today the paths by which toxic chemicals enter the ecosystem and their effects are just beginning to be understood. Finally, the authors take us through the ways in which governments have sought to understand and respond to the many difficult questions facing the lakes, from the advent of the Boundary Waters Treaty of 1909 to our present day Great Lakes Water Quality Agreement.

It is imperative that we understand what has happened to the lakes over time in order to come to grips with the problems we are facing today. It is our hope that this atlas will provide all our citizens with the grounding they need to be full participants in resolving the problems facing our lakes. Future generations depend on us to do so.

Tom McMillan, PC MP
Minister of the Environment

Lee M. Thomas
Administrator,
U.S. Environmental Protection Agency

Environment Environnement
Canada Canada

RELIEF, DRAINAGE AND URBAN AREAS

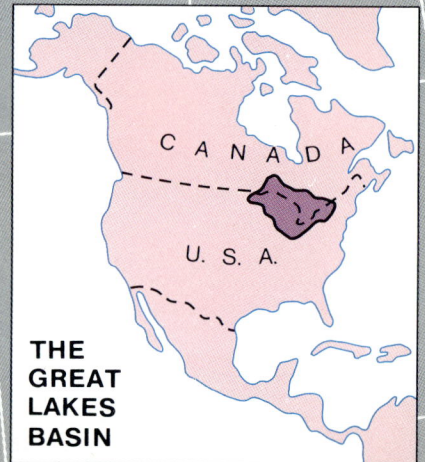

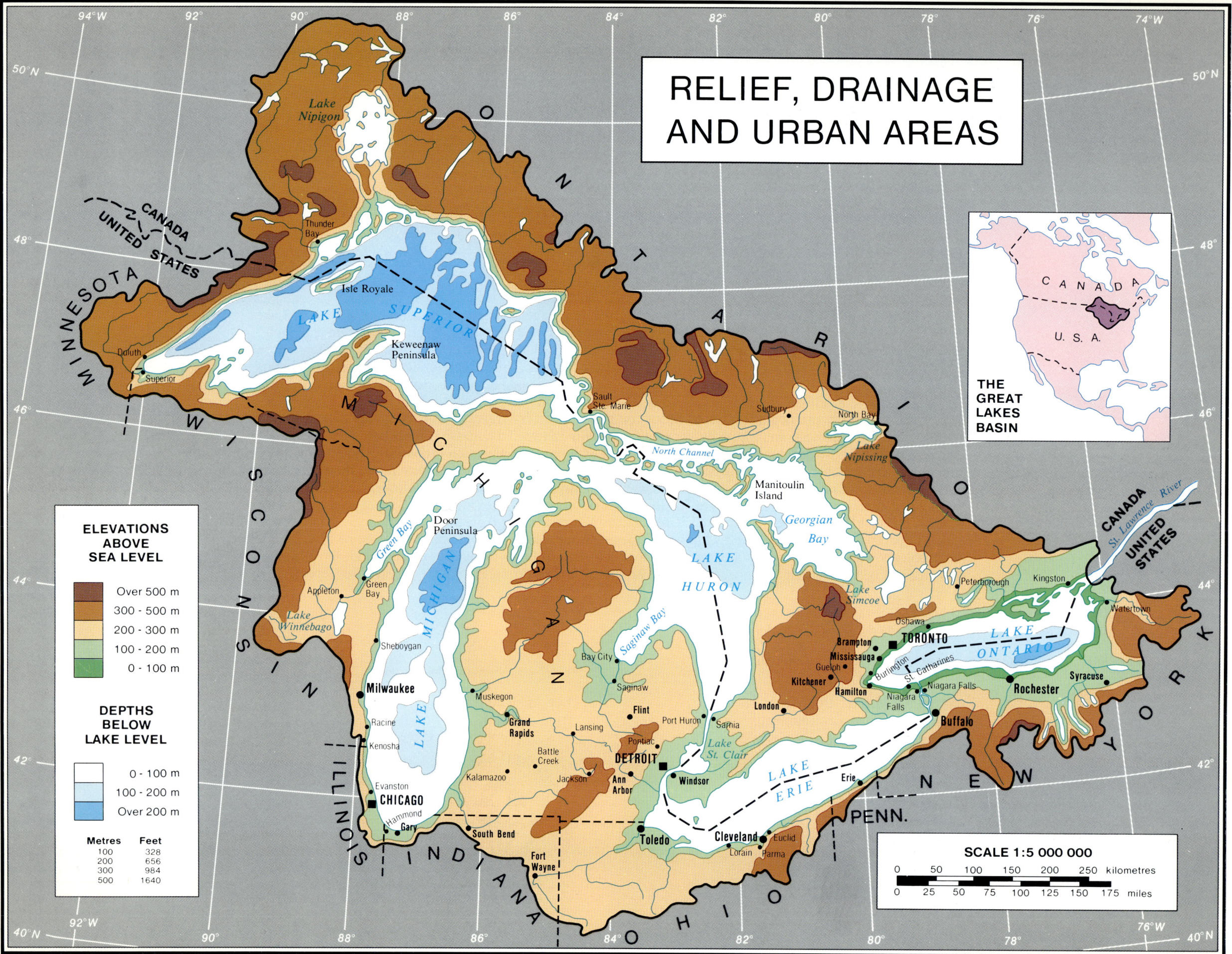

THE GREAT LAKES BASIN

ELEVATIONS ABOVE SEA LEVEL

- Over 500 m
- 300 - 500 m
- 200 - 300 m
- 100 - 200 m
- 0 - 100 m

DEPTHS BELOW LAKE LEVEL

- 0 - 100 m
- 100 - 200 m
- Over 200 m

Metres	Feet
100	328
200	656
300	984
500	1640

SCALE 1:5 000 000

0   50   100   150   200   250 kilometres

0   25   50   75   100   125   150   175 miles

MINNESOTA

CANADA

UNITED STATES

Lake Nipigon

Thunder Bay

Duluth

Superior

WISCONSIN

Isle Royale

LAKE SUPERIOR

Keweenaw Peninsula

Sault Ste. Marie

ONTARIO

Sudbury

North Bay

Lake Nipissing

North Channel

Manitoulin Island

Georgian Bay

Lake Simcoe

Peterborough

Kingston

Watertown

St. Lawrence River

CANADA

UNITED STATES

Green Bay

Door Peninsula

MICHIGAN

LAKE HURON

Saginaw Bay

Appleton

Green Bay

Lake Winnebago

Sheboygan

LAKE MICHIGAN

Bay City

Saginaw

Milwaukee

Muskegon

Racine

Grand Rapids

Lansing

Flint

Port Huron

Sarnia

London

Kenosha

Battle Creek

Kalamazoo

Jackson

Pontiac

Ann Arbor

DETROIT

Windsor

Lake St. Clair

Oshawa

Brampton

Mississauga

Guelph

Kitchener

Hamilton

Burlington

St. Catharines

Niagara Falls

Niagara Falls

TORONTO

LAKE ONTARIO

Rochester

Syracuse

Buffalo

LAKE ERIE

Erie

Erie

ILLINOIS

Evanston

CHICAGO

Hammond

Gary

South Bend

INDIANA

Fort Wayne

Toledo

OHIO

Cleveland

Euclid

Lorain

Parma

PENN.

NEW YORK

Brock University Cartography

CHAPTER ONE

INTRODUCTION: THE GREAT LAKES

The Great Lakes - Superior, Michigan, Huron, Erie and Ontario - are an important part of the physical and cultural heritage of North America. Spanning more than 1,200 kilometres (750 miles) from west to east, these vast inland freshwater seas have provided water for consumption, transportation, power, recreation and a host of other uses.

The water of the lakes and the many resources of the Great Lakes basin have played a major role in the history and development of the United States and Canada. For the early European explorers and settlers, the lakes and their tributaries were the avenues for penetrating the continent, extracting valued resources and carrying local products abroad.

Now the Great Lakes basin is home to more than one-tenth of the population of the United States and one-quarter of the people of Canada. Some of the world's largest concentrations of industrial capacity are located in the Great Lakes region. Nearly 25 percent of the total Canadian agricultural production and seven percent of the American production are located in the basin. The United States considers the Great Lakes a fourth seacoast and the Great Lakes region is a dominant factor in the Canadian industrial economy.

Physical Characteristics of the System

The magnitude of the Great Lakes water system is difficult to appreciate, even for those who live within the basin. As a whole, the lakes contain about 23,000 km³ (5,500 cu. mi.) of water covering a total area of 244,000 km²(94,000 sq. mi.) The Great Lakes are the largest system of fresh, surface water on earth, containing roughly 18 percent of the world supply. Only the polar ice caps contain more fresh water.

In spite of their large size, the Great Lakes are sensitive to the effects of a wide range of pollutants. The sources of pollution include the runoff of soils and farm chemicals from agricultural lands, the waste from cities, discharges from industrial areas, and leachate from disposal sites. The large surface area of the lakes also makes them vulnerable to direct atmospheric pollutants that fall with rain or snow and as dust on the lake surface.

Outflows from the Great Lakes are relatively small (less than one percent per year) in comparison to the total volume of water. Pollutants that enter the lakes - whether by direct discharge along the shores, through tributaries, from land use, or from the atmosphere - are retained in the system and become more concentrated with time. Also, pollutants remain in the system because of resuspension (or mixing back into the water) of sediment and cycling through biological food chains.

Because of the large size of the watershed, physical

characteristics such as climate, soils and topography vary across the basin. To the north the climate is cold and the terrain is dominated by a granite bedrock called the Canadian (or Laurentian) Shield consisting of Precambrian rocks under a generally thin layer of acidic soils. Conifers dominate the northern forests.

In the southern areas of the basin the climate is much warmer. The soils are deeper with layers or mixtures of clays, silts, sands, gravels and boulders deposited as glacial drift or as glacial lake and river sediments. The lands are usually fertile and can be readily drained for agriculture. The original deciduous forests have given way to agriculture and sprawling urban development.

Although part of a single system, each lake is different. In volume, Lake Superior is the largest. It is also the deepest and coldest of the five. Superior could contain all the other Great Lakes and three more Lake Eries. Because of its size, Superior has a retention time of 191 years. Retention time is a measure based on the volume of water in the lake and the mean rate of outflow. Most of the Superior basin is forested with little agriculture due to a cool climate and poor soils. Because of the forests and the sparse population, relatively few pollutants enter Lake Superior, except through airborne transport.

Lake Michigan, the second largest, is the only Great Lake

The northern region of the Great Lakes is sparsely populated and is characterized by coniferous forests and rocky shorelines. Above, the western shore of Georgian Bay in the Bruce Peninsula National Park.

entirely within the United States. The northern part is in the colder, less developed upper Great Lakes region. It is sparsely populated, except for the Fox River Valley which drains into Green Bay. This bay has one of the most productive Great Lakes fisheries but receives the wastes from the world's largest concentration of pulp and paper mills. The more temperate southern basin of Lake Michigan is among the most urbanized areas in the Great Lakes system. It contains the Milwaukee and Chicago metropolitan areas. This region is home to about 8 million people or about one-fifth of the total population of the Great Lakes basin.

Lake Huron, which includes Georgian Bay, is the third largest of the lakes by volume. Many Canadians and Americans own cottages on the shallow, sandy beaches of Huron and along the rocky shores of Georgian Bay. The Saginaw River basin is intensively farmed and contains the Flint and Saginaw-Bay City metropolitan areas. Saginaw Bay, like Green Bay, contains a very productive fishery.

Lake Erie is the smallest of the lakes in volume and is exposed to the greatest effects from urbanization and agriculture. Because of the fertile soils surrounding the lake, the area is intensively farmed. The lake receives runoff from the agricultural area of southwestern Ontario and parts of Ohio, Indiana and Michigan. Seventeen metropolitan areas of over 50,000 population are located within the Lake Erie basin. Although the area of the lake is about 26,000 km² (10,000 sq. mi.), the average depth is only about 19 metres (62 feet). It is the shallowest and therefore warms rapidly in the spring and summer and frequently freezes over in winter. It also has the shortest retention time of the lakes, 2.6 years. The western basin, comprising about one-fifth of the lake, is very shallow with an average depth of 7.4 metres (24 feet) and a maximum depth of 19 metres (62 feet).

Lake Ontario, although slightly smaller in area, is much deeper than its upstream neighbor, Lake Erie, with an average depth of 86 metres (283 feet) and a retention time of about 6 years. Major urban industrial centers, such as Hamilton and Toronto are located on its shore. The U.S. shore is less urbanized and is not intensively farmed, except for a narrow band along the lake.

Settlement

The modern history of the Great Lakes region, from discovery and settlement by European immigrants to the present day, can be viewed not only as a progression of intensifying use of a vast natural resource, but also as a process of learning about the Great Lakes ecosystem. At first it was a matter of learning to make use of the natural resources of the basin while avoiding its dangers. Not until much later, when the watershed was more intensively settled and exploited, was it learned that abuse of the waters and the basin could result in great damage to the entire system.

Exploitation

The first Europeans found a relatively stable ecosystem which had evolved during the 10,000 years since the retreat of the last glacier; a system that was only moderately disturbed by the hunting and agricultural activities of the native peoples. The first arrivals had a modest impact on the system, limited to the exploitation of some fur-bearing animals. However, the following waves of immigrants logged, farmed and fished commercially in the region, bringing about profound ecological changes. The mature forests were clearcut from the watersheds, soil was laid bare by the plow, and the undisturbed fish populations were harvested indiscriminately by an awesome new predator - men with nets.

As settlement and exploitation intensified, portions of the system were drastically changed. Logging removed protective shade from streams and left them blocked with debris. Sawmills left streams and embayments clogged with sawdust. When the land was plowed for farming the exposed soils washed away more readily, burying valuable stream and river mouth habitats. Exploitive fishing began to reduce the seemingly endless abundance of fish stocks and whole populations of fish began to disappear.

Great Lakes Factsheet No. 1
Physical Features and Population

	Superior	Michigan	Huron	Erie	Ontario	Totals
Elevation[a] (feet)**	600	577	577	569	243	
(metres)	183	176	176	173	74	
Length (miles)*	350	307	206	241	193	
(kilometres)	563	494	332	388	311	
Breadth (miles)*	160	118	183	57	53	
(kilometres)	257	190	245	92	85	
Average Depth[a] (feet)**	483	279	195	62	283	
(metres)	147	85	59	19	86	
Maximum Depth[a] (feet)*	1,330	923	750	210	802	
(metres)	405	281	229	64	244	
Volume[a] (cu. miles)*	2,900	1,180	850	116	393	5,439
(km³)	12,100	4,920	3,540	484	1,640	22,684
Area:						
Water (sq. mi.)*	31,700	22,300	23,000	9,910	7,340	94,250
(km²)	82,100	57,800	59,600	25,700	18,960	244,160
Land Drainage Area[b] (sq. mi.)*	49,300	45,600	51,700	30,140	24,720	201,460
(km²)	127,700	118,000	134,100	78,000	64,030	521,830
Total (sq. mi.)*	81,000	67,900	74,700	40,050	32,060	295,710
(km²)	209,800	175,800	193,700	103,700	82,990	765,990
Shoreline Length[c] (miles)*	2,726	1,638	3,827	871	712	10,210[d]
(kilometres)	4,385	2,633	6,157	1,402	1,146	17,017[d]
Retention Time (years)**	191	99	22	2.6	6	
Population: U.S. (1980)	558,100	13,970,900	1,321,000	11,347,500	2,090,300	29,287,800
Canada (1981)	180,440		1,051,119	1,621,106	4,551,875	7,404,540
Totals	738,540	13,970,900	2,372,119	12,968,606	6,642,175	36,692,340
Outlet	St. Marys River	Straits of Mackinac	St. Clair River	Niagara River Welland Canal	St. Lawrence River	

Notes:

[a] Measured at Low Water Datum.

[b] Land Drainage Area for: Lake Huron includes the St. Mary s River.
Lake Erie includes the St. Clair-Detroit system.
Lake Ontario includes the Niagara River.

[c] Including islands.

[d] These totals are greater than the sum of the shoreline length for the lakes because they include the connecting channels (excluding the St. Lawrence River).

Sources: *Coordinating Committee on Great Lakes Basic Hydraulic and Hydrologic Data, COORDINATED GREAT LAKES PHYSICAL DATA. May, 1977.
**EXTENSION BULLETINS E-1866-70, Michigan Sea Grant College Program, Cooperative Extension Service, Michigan State University, E. Lansing, Michigan, 1985.

Industrialization

Industrialization followed close behind agrarian settlement and the virtually untreated wastes of early industrialization degraded one river after another. The growing urbanization that accompanied industrial development added to the degradation of water quality, creating nuisance conditions such as bacterial contamination, putrescence and floating debris in rivers and nearshore areas. Some of the situations caused fatal epidemics of waterborne disease such as typhoid. Nonetheless, the problems were perceived as being local in nature.

As industrialization progressed, and as agriculture intensified following the turn of the century, new chemical substances came into use, such as PCBs (polychlorinated biphenyls) in the 1920s and DDT (dichlorodiphenyl-trichloroethane) in the 1940s. Non-organic fertilizers were used to enrich the already fertile soil to enhance production. The combination of synthetic fertilizers, existing sources of nutrient-rich organic pollutants such as untreated human wastes from cities, and phosphate detergents caused an acceleration of biological production (eutrophication) in the lakes. In the 1950s, Lake Erie showed the first evidence of lake-wide eutrophic imbalance with massive algal blooms and the depletion of oxygen.

The Evolution of Great Lakes Management

In the late 1960s, growing public concern about the deterioration of water quality in the Great Lakes stimulated new investment in pollution research especially the problems of eutrophication and DDT. Governments responded to the concern by controlling and regulating pollutant discharges and assisting with the construction of municipal sewage treatment works. This concern was formalized in the first Great Lakes Water Quality Agreement between Canada and the U.S. in 1972.

Major reductions were made in pollutant discharges in the 1970s. The results were visible. Nuisance conditions occurred less frequently as floating debris and oil slicks began to disappear. Dissolved oxygen levels improved, eliminating odor problems. Many beaches reopened as a result of improved sewage control and algal mats disappeared as nutrient levels declined. The initiatives of the 1970s showed that improvements could be made and provided several important lessons beyond the cleanup of localized nuisance conditions.

First, the problem of algal growth in the lakes caused by accelerated eutrophication required a lake-wide approach to measure the amount of the critical nutrient, phosphorus, entering and leaving each lake from all sources and outlets. This approach of calculating a 'mass balance' of the substance was then combined with research and mathematical modeling to set target loading limits for phosphorus entering the lake (or

Industrialization of the Great Lakes basin followed early settlement and the growth in agriculture. Above, a river winds its way through an industrial city in the basin. (ca. 1970)

portions of the lake). The target load is the amount that will not cause excessive algal growth (i.e., an amount that could safely be assimilated by the ecosystem).

Other major lessons learned about the system arose as a result of research on toxic substances, initially the pesticide DDT. Toxic contaminants include persistent organic chemicals and metals. These substances enter the lakes in direct discharges of sewage and industrial effluents and indirectly from waste sites, diffuse land runoff and by atmospheric deposition. As a result of increased research, sampling and surveillance, toxic substances have been found to be a system-wide problem.

Research showed that some toxic substances biologically accumulate throughout the food chain. Consequently top predators such as lake trout and fish-eating birds - cormorants, ospreys and herring gulls - suffer adverse effects. Because of biological accumulation, concentrations of toxic substances can be a million times higher in fish than in water. Therefore, the potential for human exposure to the contaminants is far greater from fish consumption than from drinking lake water. Although there is uncertainty about the risk to human health of long-term exposure to low levels of toxic pollutants in the

lakes, there is no disagreement that the risk to human health will increase if toxic contaminants continue to accumulate in the Great Lakes ecosystem. These concepts - mass balance, system-wide contamination and bioaccumulation in the food chain - have become essential components in understanding the lakes from an ecosystem perspective.

The second Great Lakes Water Quality Agreement was signed in 1978. Canada and the U.S. recognized that understanding the interconnected nature of the system required an ecosystem approach. Learning about the Great Lakes has continued since the signing of the 1978 Agreement. The mass balance approach to phosphorus control has been used to formulate target pollutant loadings for the lower lakes. The understanding of toxic contamination continues to evolve rapidly as a result of continued monitoring and research. From the research it appears that, although present pollution is not as visually dramatic as earlier forms (except possibly for fish tumors and bird deformities), the less visible toxic impacts may actually be causing far greater system-wide damage to the life in the lakes in the form of impaired reproduction, disrupted and contaminated food chains, and genetic change. Continued research is needed to better understand the sources, pathways, impacts and effective control methods of toxic contaminants.

It is clear that disruption of the Great Lakes ecosystem will continue for the forseeable future. The ecosystem focus of the Great Lakes Water Quality Agreement, the growing use of the mass balance approach, and the awareness of the need to address multiple contaminants offer the hope of continuing progress toward a successful strategy for reducing toxics and 'decontaminating' the Great Lakes ecosystem.

The 36 million people who live in the Great Lakes basin, and their governments, face an immense challenge for the future of the basin. The wise management needed to maintain the use of Great Lakes resources requires greater public awareness, the forging of political will to protect the lakes, and creative government action and cooperation. It will not be easy.

The Great Lakes are surrounded by two sovereign nations, a Canadian province, eight American states and thousands of local, regional and special-purpose governing bodies with jurisdiction for management of some aspect of the basin or the lakes. Cooperation is essential because problems such as water consumption, diversions, lake levels and shoreline management - like the problem of pollution - do not respect political boundaries.

Humans are part of, and depend on, the natural ecosystem of the Great Lakes, but are damaging the capacity of the system to renew and sustain itself and the life within it. Protection of the lakes for future use requires a greater understanding of how past problems developed as well as continued remedial action to prevent further damage.

GEOLOGY AND MINERAL RESOURCES

STAGES IN THE EVOLUTION OF THE GREAT LAKES

SCALE 1 : 20 000 000

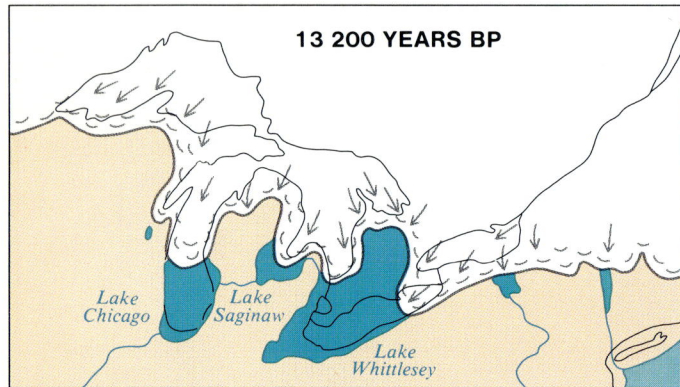

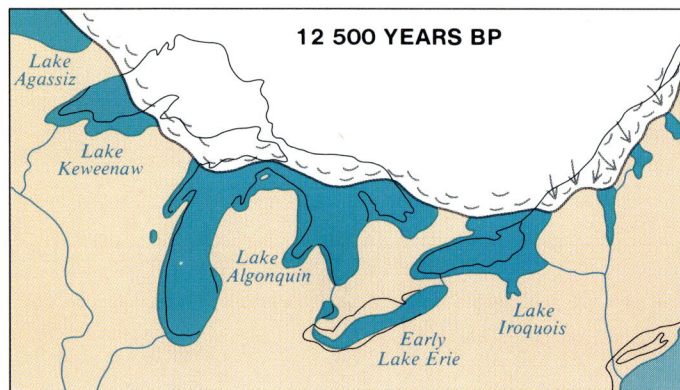

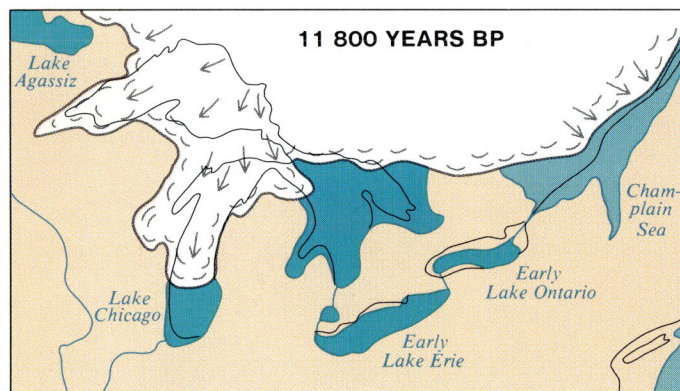

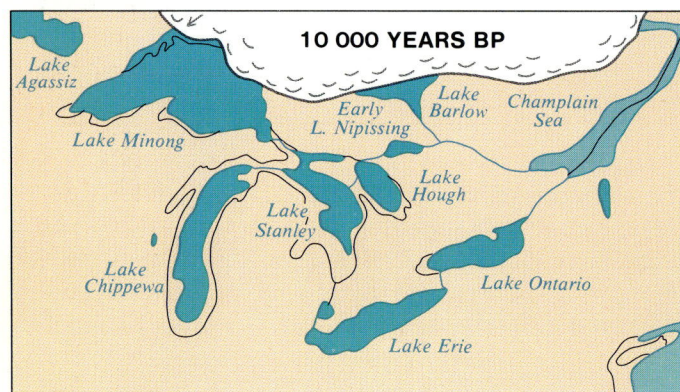

13 200 YEARS BP

Lake Chicago
Lake Saginaw
Lake Whittlesey

12 500 YEARS BP

Lake Agassiz
Lake Keweenaw
Lake Algonquin
Early Lake Erie
Lake Iroquois

11 800 YEARS BP

Lake Agassiz
Lake Chicago
Early Lake Erie
Early Lake Ontario
Champlain Sea

10 000 YEARS BP

Lake Agassiz
Lake Minong
Lake Chippewa
Lake Stanley
Lake Hough
Early L. Nipissing
Lake Barlow
Champlain Sea
Lake Ontario
Lake Erie

NOTE:
The maps on left are "snapshots" of a continuously changing situation during the retreat of the Wisconsin icesheet. They should not be viewed as a simple sequence, since many intermediate stages are omitted. The letters BP denote before present.

Legend

- Ice
- Ice Front
- Advancing Ice
- Fresh Water
- Salt Water
- Present Coastline

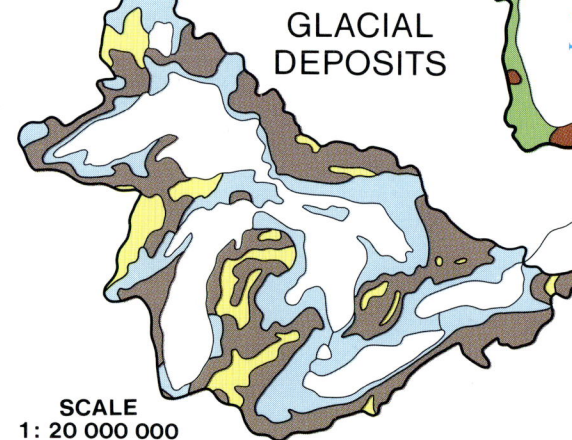

SCALE 1 : 7 500 000

0   100   200   300   kilometres
0   50   100   150   200   miles

Lake Superior
Lake Michigan
Lake Huron
Lake Erie
Lake Ontario

A
B

GLACIAL DEPOSITS

SCALE 1 : 20 000 000

Stratified Drift

- Silt and Clay (glacial lake deposits)
- Sand and Gravel (outwash, alluvial and ice contact deposits)

Unstratified Drift

- Till (ground and end moraines)

Bedrock areas where the glacial cover is absent (e.g. parts of Canadian Shield) are not distinguished.

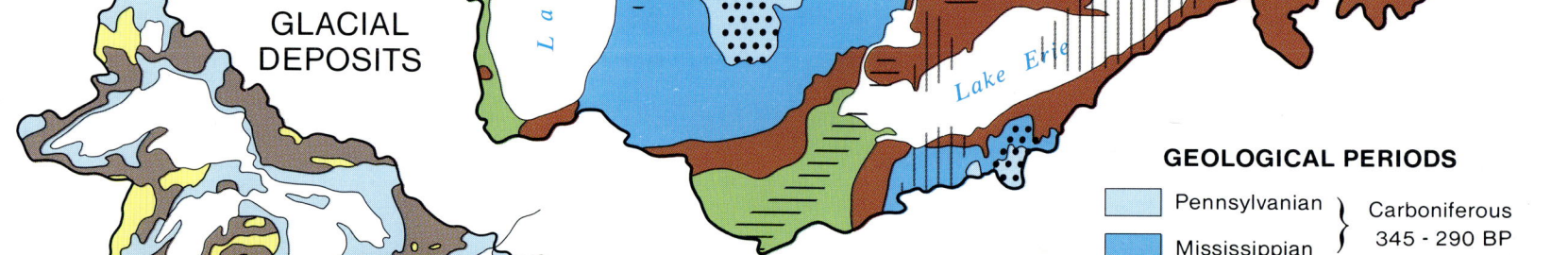

PRINCIPAL MINERAL AREAS

- Coal
- Gas
- Oil
- Uranium
- Copper & Zinc
- Gold & Silver
- Iron Ore
- Nickel

The extraction of minerals such as sand, gravel and limestone is widespread and not mappable at this scale. Other minerals, such as salt and gypsum, are omitted to preserve clarity.

GEOLOGICAL PERIODS

Period	Age
Pennsylvanian	Carboniferous 345 - 290 BP
Mississippian	Carboniferous 345 - 290 BP
Devonian	400 - 345 BP
Silurian	440 - 400 BP
Ordovician	500 - 440 BP
Cambrian	570 - 500 BP
Precambrian	4500 - 570 BP

Figures denote age in millions of years before present (BP).

GENERALIZED CROSS-SECTION

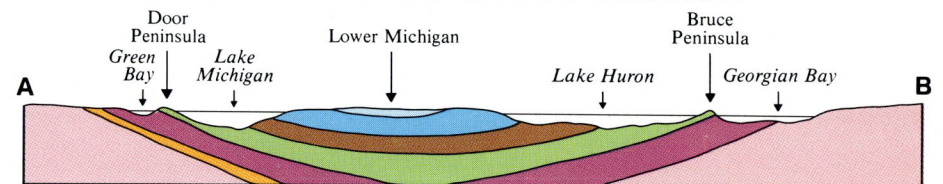

A
Door Peninsula
Green Bay
Lake Michigan
Lower Michigan
Lake Huron
Bruce Peninsula
Georgian Bay
B

Brock University Cartography

CHAPTER TWO   NATURAL PROCESSES IN THE GREAT LAKES

GEOLOGY

The foundation for the present Great Lakes basin was set about three billion years ago during the Precambrian Era. This era occupies about five-sixths of all geological time and was a period of great volcanic activity and tremendous stresses which formed great mountain systems. Early sedimentary and volcanic rocks were folded and heated (metamorphosed) into complex structures. These were later eroded and, today, appear as the gently rolling hills and small mountain remnants of the Canadian Shield which forms the northern and northwestern portions of the Great Lakes basin. Granitic rocks of the shield extend southward beneath the Paleozoic sedimentary rocks where they form the 'basement' structure of the southern and eastern portions of the basin.

With the coming of the Paleozoic Era, most of central North America was flooded again and again by marine seas which were inhabited by a multitude of life forms, including corals, crinoids, brachiopods and mollusks. The seas deposited lime muds, clays, sand and salts which eventually consolidated into limestone, shales, sandstone, halite and gypsum.

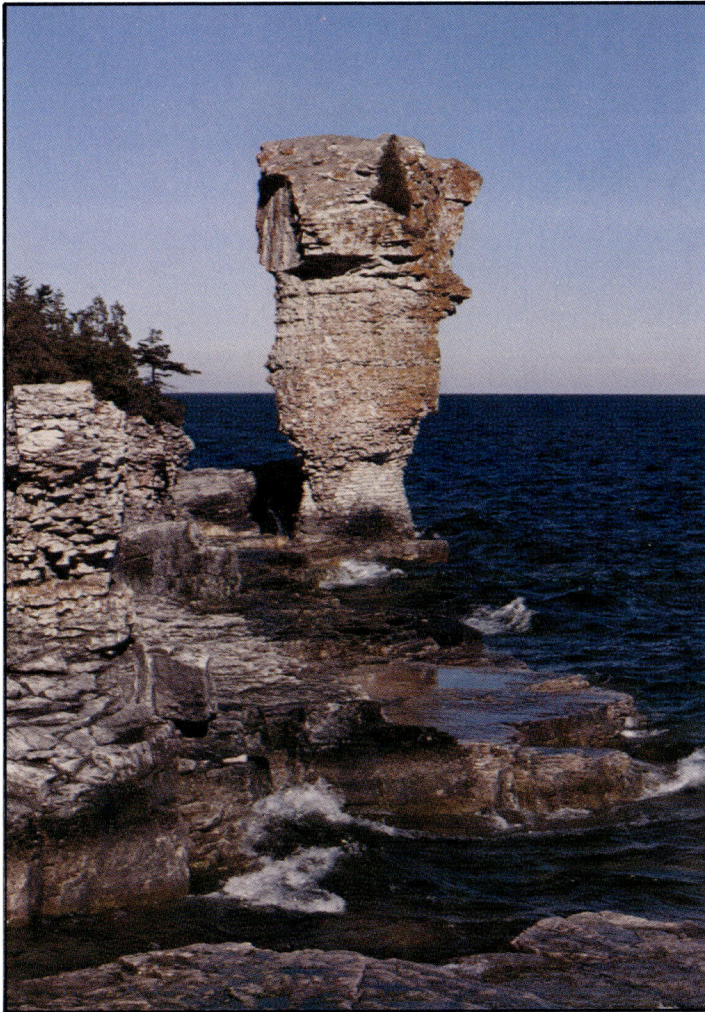

During the Pleistocene epoch, the continental glaciers repeatedly advanced over the Great Lakes region from the north. The first glacier began to advance more than a million years ago. As they inched forward, the glaciers, up to 2,000 metres (6,500 feet) thick, scoured the surface of the earth, leveled hills, and altered forever the previous ecosystem. Valleys created by the river systems of the previous era were deepened and enlarged to form the basins for the Great Lakes. Thousands of years later, the climate began to warm, melting and slowly shrinking the glacier. This was followed by an interglacial period during which vegetation and wildlife returned. The whole cycle was repeated several times.

Sand, silt, clay and boulders deposited by the glacier occur in various mixtures and forms. These deposits are collectively referred to as 'glacial drift' and include features such as moraines, which are linear mounds of poorly sorted material or 'till', flat till plains, till drumlins, and eskers formed of well-sorted sands and gravels deposited from meltwater. Areas having substantial deposits of well-sorted sands and gravels (eskers, kames and outwash) are usually significant groundwater storage and transmission areas called 'aquifers'. These also serve as excellent sources of sand and gravel for commercial extraction.

As the last glacier retreated, large volumes of meltwater occurred along the front of the ice. Because the land was greatly depressed at this time from the weight of the glacier, large glacial lakes formed. These lakes were much larger than the present Great Lakes. Their legacy can still be seen in the form of beach ridges, eroded bluffs and flat plains located high above present lake levels. Glacial lake plains known as lacustrine plains, occur around Saginaw Bay and west and north of Lake Erie.

Layers of sedimentary rock eroded by wind and wave action are revealed in these formations at Flower Pot Island at the tip of the Bruce Peninsula in Canada.

GEOLOGIC TIME CHART. The Great Lakes basin is a relatively young ecosystem having formed during the last 10,000 years. Its foundation was laid through many millions of years and several geologic eras. This chart gives a relative idea of the age of the eras.

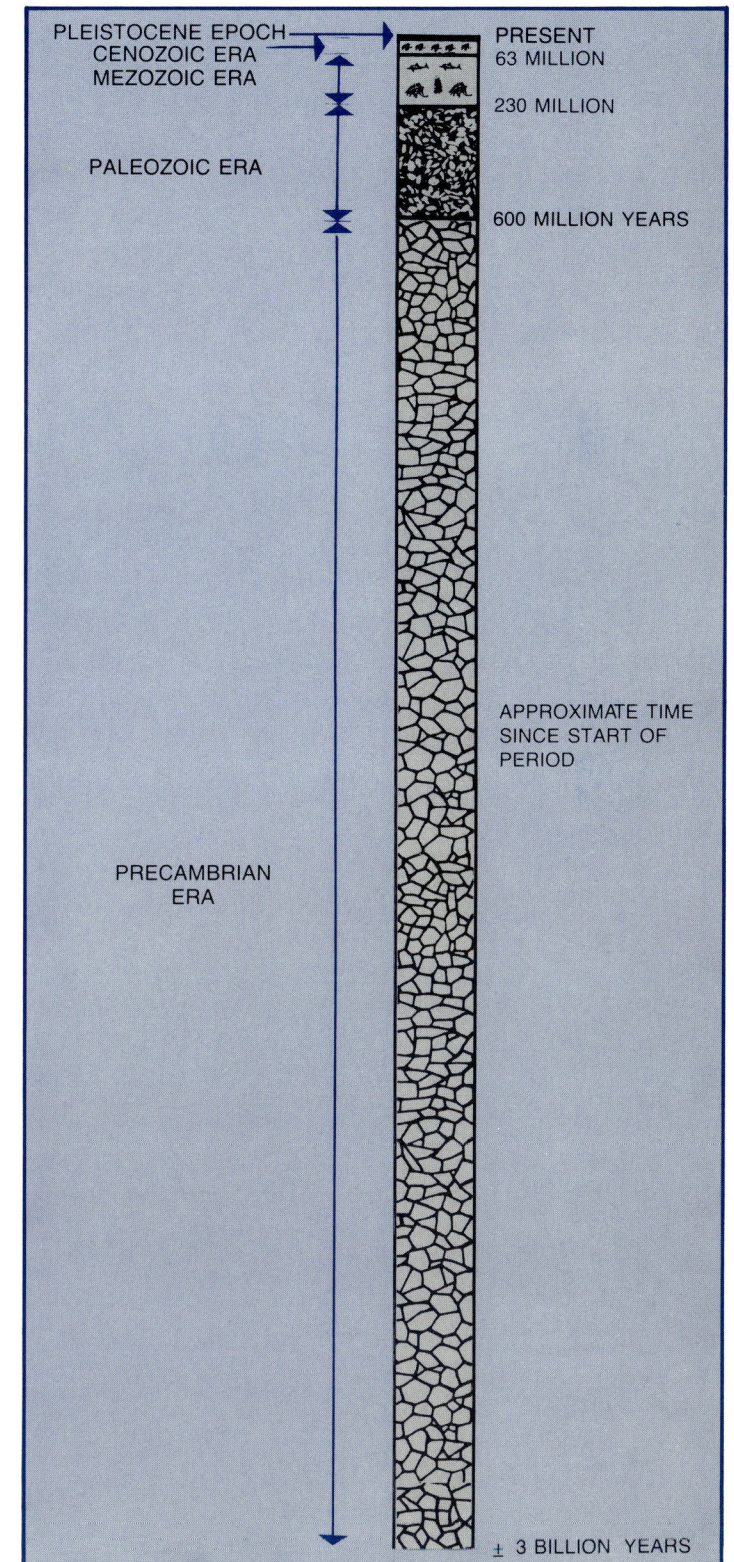

PLEISTOCENE EPOCH
CENOZOIC ERA
MEZOZOIC ERA

PRESENT
63 MILLION

230 MILLION

PALEOZOIC ERA

600 MILLION YEARS

APPROXIMATE TIME SINCE START OF PERIOD

PRECAMBRIAN ERA

± 3 BILLION YEARS

WINTER TEMPERATURES AND ICE CONDITIONS

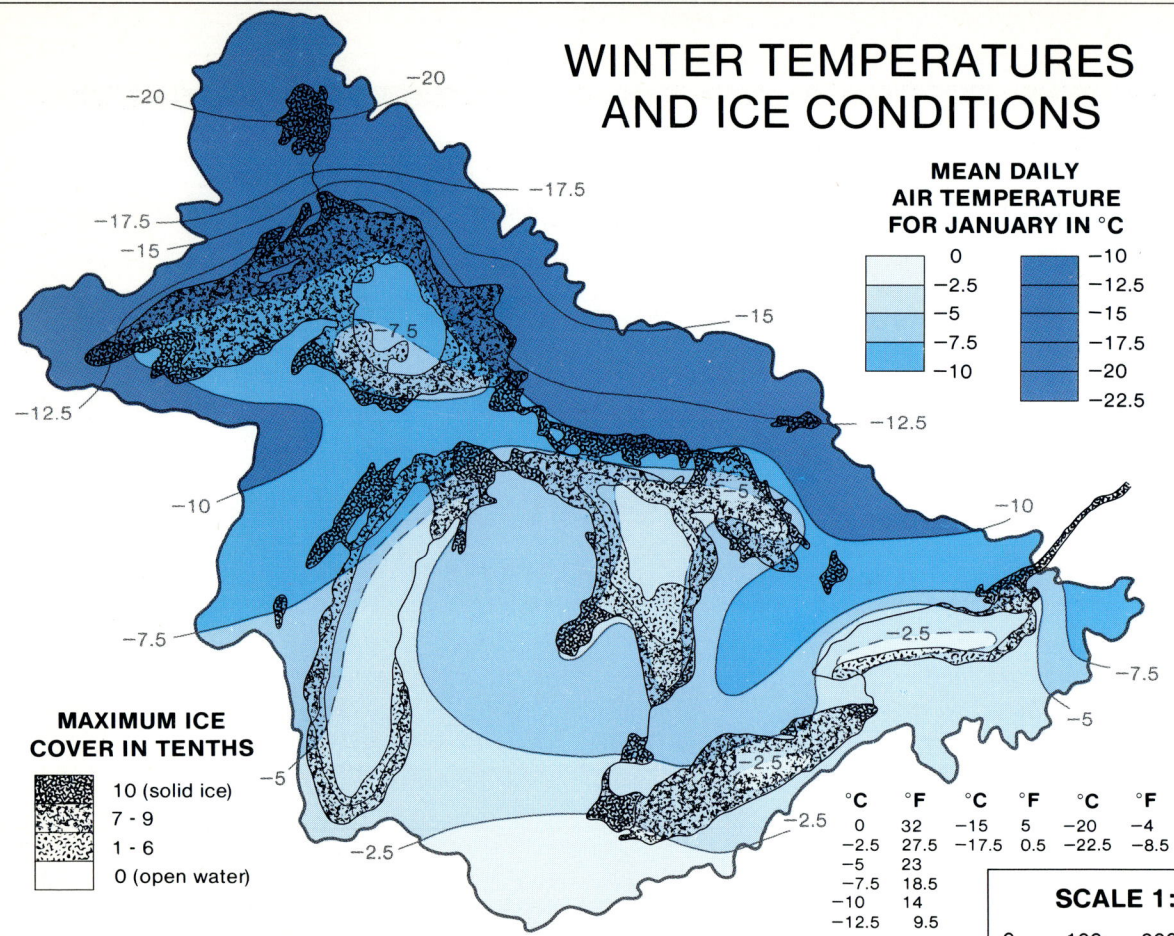

MEAN DAILY AIR TEMPERATURE FOR JANUARY IN °C

0	−10
−2.5	−12.5
−5	−15
−7.5	−17.5
−10	−20
	−22.5

Isotherm labels: −20, −17.5, −15, −12.5, −10, −7.5, −5, −2.5

MAXIMUM ICE COVER IN TENTHS

- 10 (solid ice)
- 7 - 9
- 1 - 6
- 0 (open water)

°C	°F	°C	°F	°C	°F
0	32	−15	5	−20	−4
−2.5	27.5	−17.5	0.5	−22.5	−8.5
−5	23				
−7.5	18.5				
−10	14				
−12.5	9.5				

FROST FREE PERIOD AND AIR MASSES

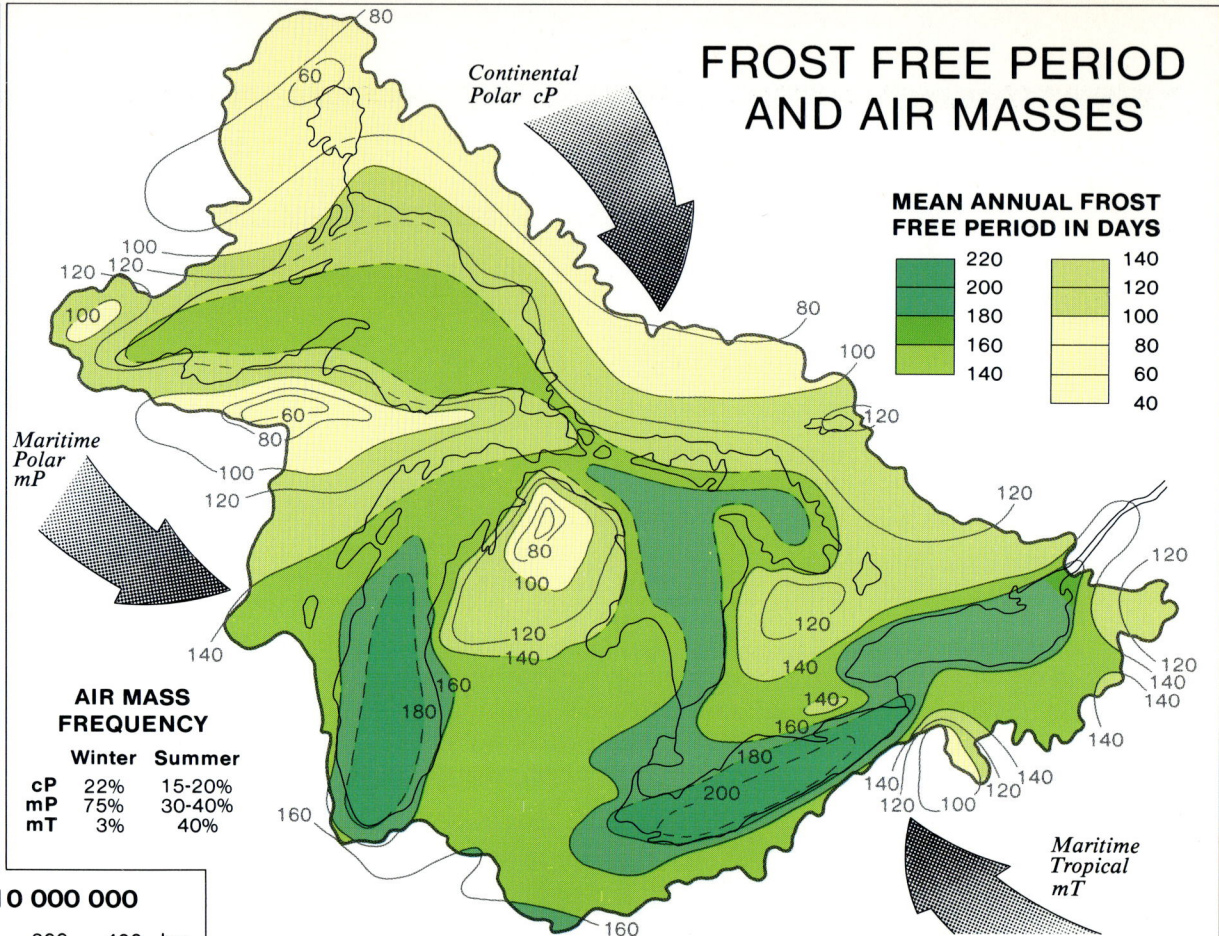

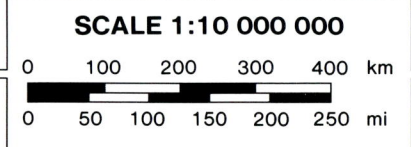

Continental Polar cP

Maritime Polar mP

Maritime Tropical mT

MEAN ANNUAL FROST FREE PERIOD IN DAYS

220	140
200	120
180	100
160	80
140	60
	40

AIR MASS FREQUENCY

	Winter	Summer
cP	22%	15-20%
mP	75%	30-40%
mT	3%	40%

SCALE 1:10 000 000

0	100	200	300	400 km
0	50	100	150	200	250 mi

SUMMER TEMPERATURES

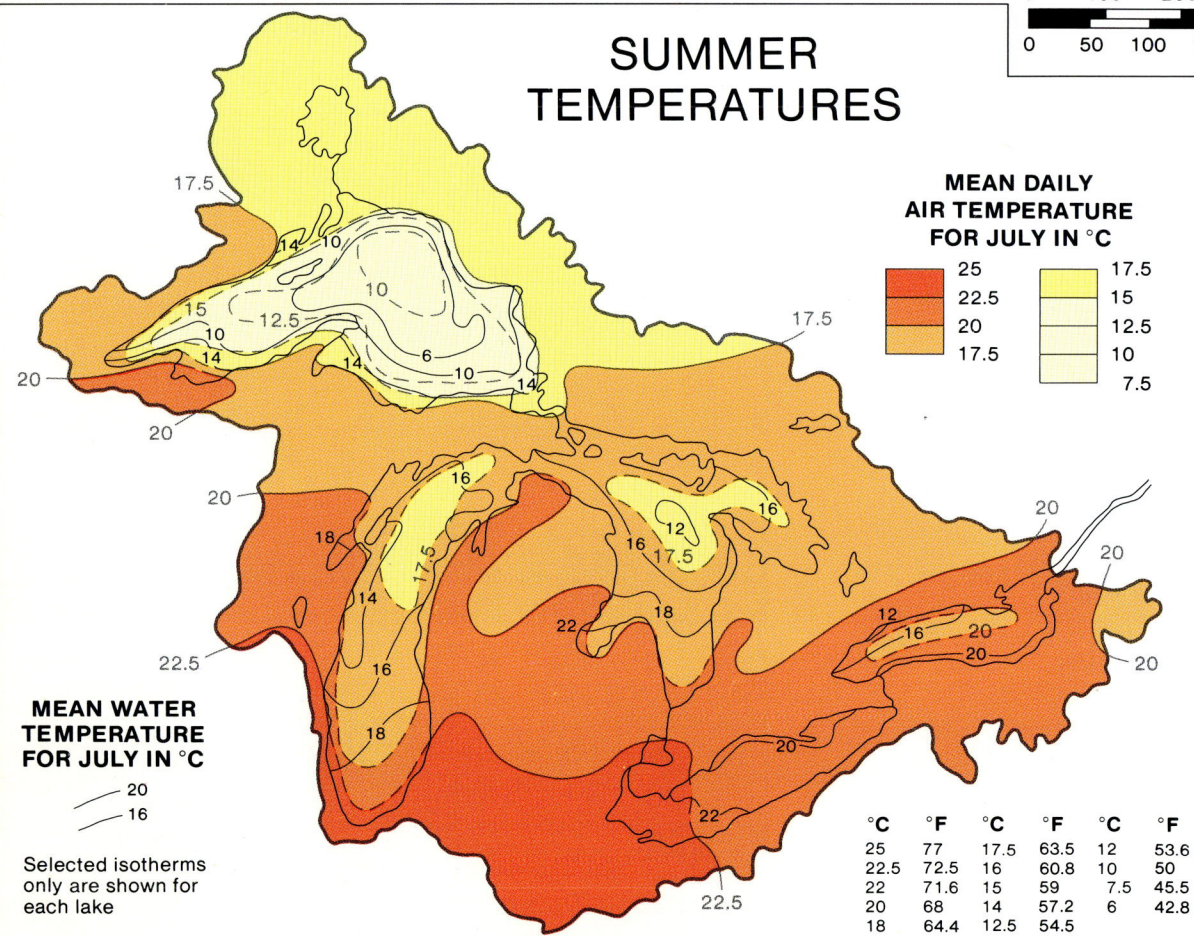

MEAN DAILY AIR TEMPERATURE FOR JULY IN °C

25	17.5
22.5	15
22	12.5
20	10
17.5	7.5

MEAN WATER TEMPERATURE FOR JULY IN °C

— 20
— 16

Selected isotherms only are shown for each lake

°C	°F	°C	°F	°C	°F
25	77	17.5	63.5	12	53.6
22.5	72.5	16	60.8	10	50
22	71.6	15	59	7.5	45.5
20	68	14	57.2	6	42.8
18	64.4	12.5	54.5		

PRECIPITATION AND SNOWBELT AREAS

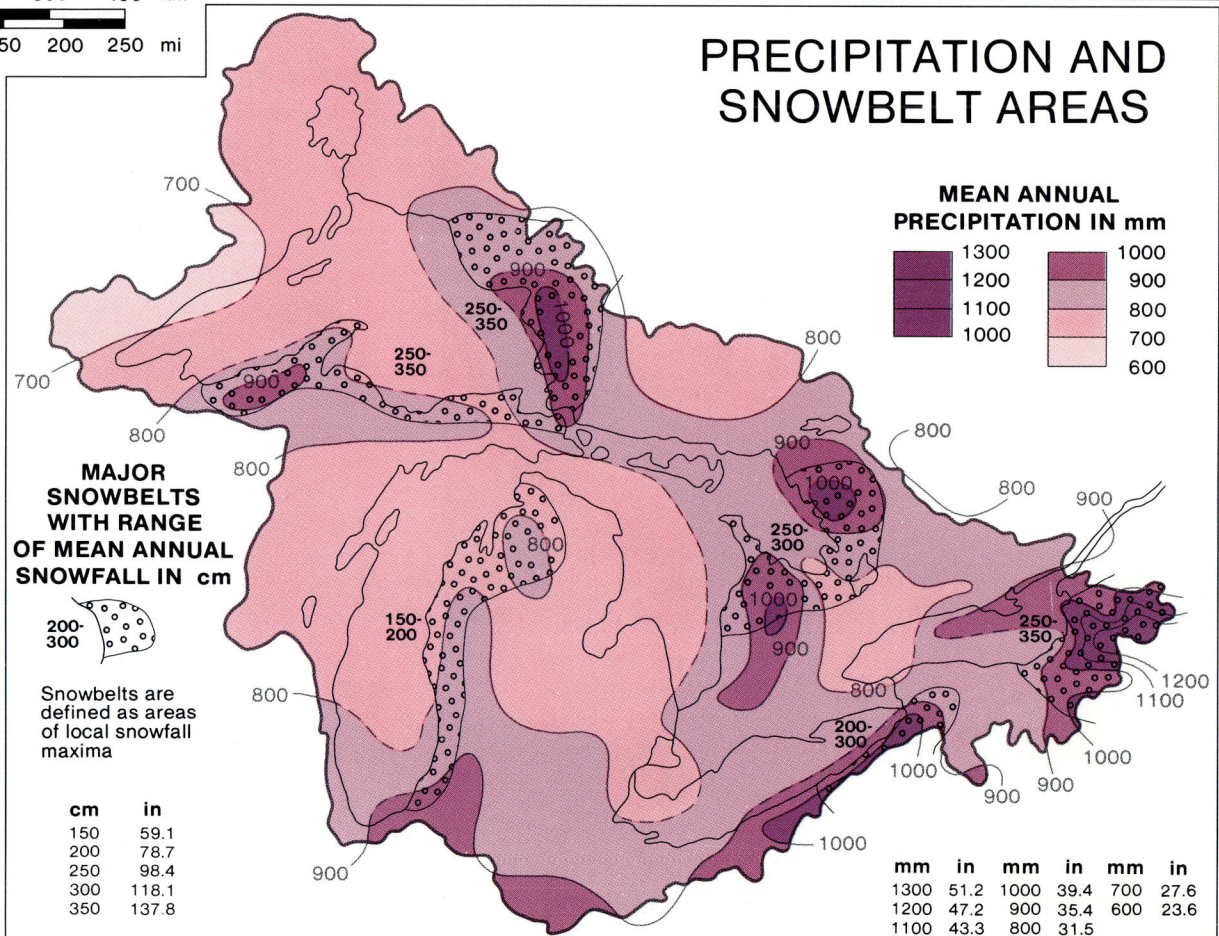

MEAN ANNUAL PRECIPITATION IN mm

1300	1000
1200	900
1100	800
1000	700
	600

MAJOR SNOWBELTS WITH RANGE OF MEAN ANNUAL SNOWFALL IN cm

200-300

Snowbelts are defined as areas of local snowfall maxima

cm	in
150	59.1
200	78.7
250	98.4
300	118.1
350	137.8

mm	in	mm	in	mm	in
1300	51.2	1000	39.4	700	27.6
1200	47.2	900	35.4	600	23.6
1100	43.3	800	31.5		

Brock University Cartography

As the glacier receded the land began to rise. This uplift (at times relatively rapid) and the shifting ice fronts caused dramatic changes in the depth, size and drainage patterns of the glacial lakes. Drainage from the lakes occurred variously through the Illinois River Valley (towards the Mississippi River), the Hudson River Valley, the Kawartha Lakes (Trent River) and the Ottawa River Valley before entering their present outlet through the St. Lawrence River Valley. Although the uplift has slowed considerably, it is still occurring in the northern portion of the basin. This, along with changing long term weather patterns, suggests that the lakes are not static and will continue to evolve.

CLIMATE

The weather in the Great Lakes basin is affected by three factors: air masses from other regions; the location of the basin within a large continental landmass; and the moderating influence of the lakes themselves. The prevailing movement of air is from the west. The characteristically changeable weather of the region is the result of alternating flows of warm, humid air from the Gulf of Mexico and cold, dry air from the Arctic.

Winter on the Lakes is characterized by alternating flows of frigid arctic air and moderating air masses from the Gulf of Mexico. Heavy snowfalls frequently occur on the lee side of the lakes.

Thousands of tributaries feed the Great Lakes, replenishing the vast supply of stored fresh water.

In summer, the northern region around Lake Superior generally receives cool dry air masses from the Canadian northwest. In the south, tropical air masses originating in the Gulf of Mexico are most influential. As the Gulf air crosses the lakes, the bottom layers remain cool while the top layers are warmed. Occasionally, the upper layer traps the cooler air below, which in turn traps moisture and airborne pollutants, and prevents them from rising and dispersing. This is called a temperature inversion and can result in dank, humid days in areas in the midst of the basin such as Michigan and Southern Ontario, and smog in low-lying industrial areas.

Increased summer sunshine warms the surface layer of water in the lakes making it lighter than the colder water below. In the fall and winter months, release of the heat stored in the lakes moderates the climate near the shores of the lakes. Parts of Southern Ontario, Michigan and Western New York enjoy milder winters than similar mid-continental areas at lower latitudes.

In the autumn, the rapid movement and occasional clash of warm and cold air masses through the region produce strong winds. Air temperatures begin to drop gradually and less sunlight, combined with increased cloudiness, signal more storms and precipitation. Late autumn storms are often the most perilous for navigation and shipping on the lakes.

In winter, the Great Lakes region is affected by two major air masses. Arctic air from the northwest is very cold and dry when it enters the basin, but is warmed and picks up moisture traveling over the comparatively warmer lakes. When it reaches the land, the moisture condenses as snow, creating heavy snowfalls on the lee side of the lakes in areas frequently referred to as snowbelts. For part of the winter, the region is affected by Pacific air masses which have lost much of their moisture crossing the western mountains. Less frequently, air masses enter the basin from the southwest bringing in moisture from the Gulf of Mexico. This air is slightly warmer and more humid. During the winter, the temperature of the lakes continues to drop. Ice frequently covers Lake Erie but seldom fully covers the other lakes.

Spring in the Great Lakes region, like autumn, is characterized by variable weather. Alternating air masses move through rapidly, resulting in frequent cloud cover and thunderstorms. By early spring, the warmer air and increased sunshine begin to melt the snow and lake ice, starting again the thermal layering of the lakes. The lakes are slower to warm than the land and tend to keep adjacent land areas cool, thus extending cool conditions sometimes well into April. In most years, this delays the leafing and blossoming of plants, protecting tender plants such as fruit trees from late frosts.

THE HYDROLOGICAL CYCLE

Water is a renewable resource. It is continually replenished in ecosystems through the hydrological cycle. Water evaporates in contact with dry air, forming water vapor. The vapor can remain as a gas, contributing to the humidity of the atmosphere, or it can condense and form water droplets which, if they remain in the air, form fog and clouds. In the Great Lakes basin much of the moisture in the region evaporates from the surface of the lakes. Other sources include the surface of small lakes and tributaries, moisture on the land mass, and water released by plants. Global movements of air also carry moisture into the basin, especially from the tropics.

Moisture-bearing air masses move through the basin and deposit their moisture as rain, snow, hail or sleet. Some of this precipitation returns to the atmosphere and some falls on the surfaces of the Great Lakes to become once again a part of the vast quantity of stored fresh water. Precipitation that falls on the land returns to the lakes as surface runoff or infiltrates the soil and becomes groundwater.

Whether it becomes surface runoff or groundwater depends upon a number of factors. Sandy soils, gravels, and some rock types contribute to groundwater flows, while clays and impermeable rocks contribute to surface runoff. Water falling on sloped areas tends to run off rapidly, while water tends to be absorbed or stored on the surface in flat areas. Vegetation also tends to decrease surface runoff; root systems hold moisture-laden soil readily and water remains on plants.

THE GREAT LAKES WATER SYSTEM

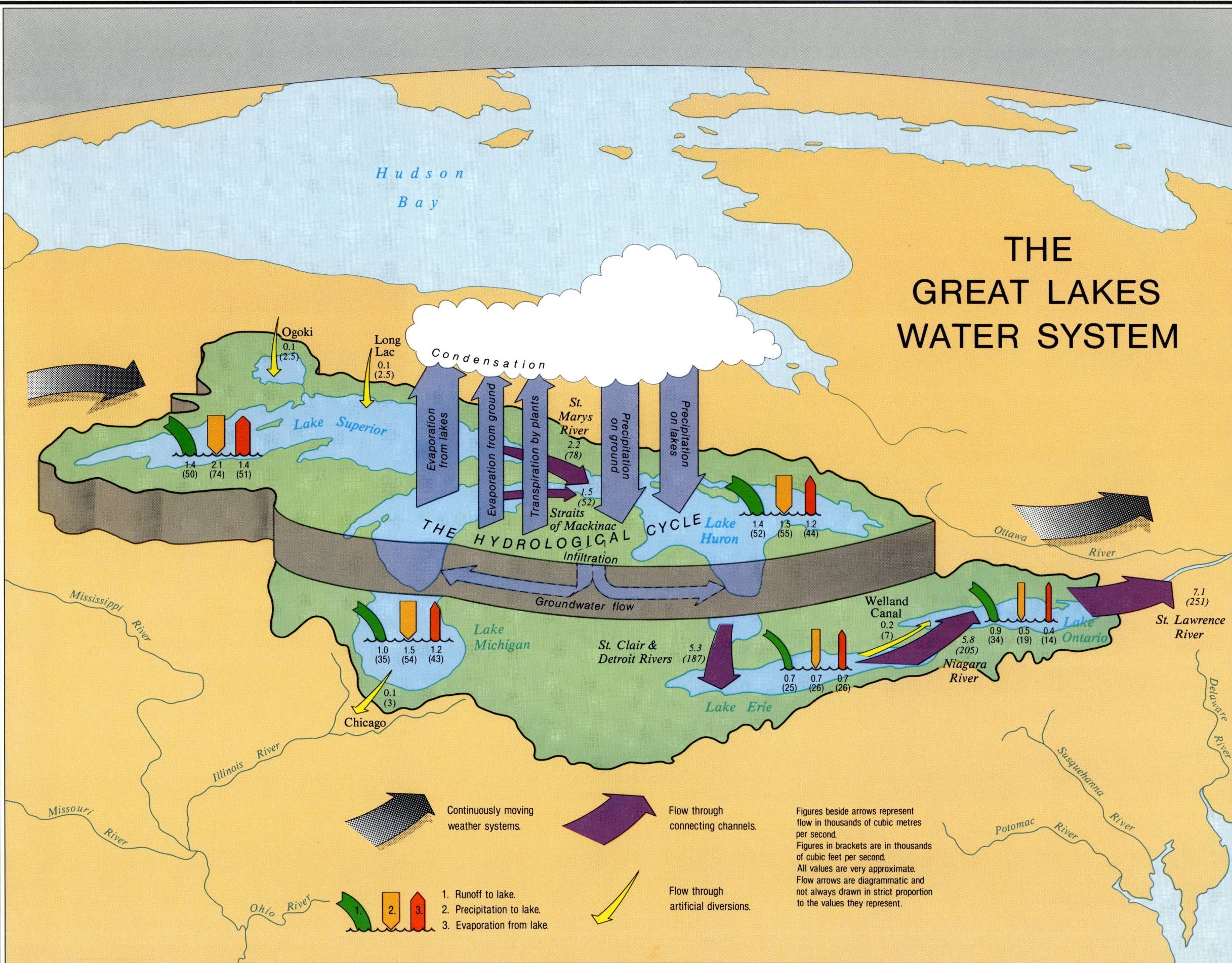

Hudson Bay

Condensation

THE HYDROLOGICAL CYCLE

Evaporation from lakes
Evaporation from ground
Transpiration by plants
Precipitation on ground
Precipitation on lakes

Ogoki
0.1
(2.5)

Long Lac
0.1
(2.5)

Lake Superior

1.4
(50)
2.1
(74)
1.4
(51)

St. Marys River
2.2
(78)

1.5
(52)

Straits of Mackinac

Lake Huron

1.4
(52)
1.5
(55)
1.2
(44)

Infiltration

Groundwater flow

Lake Michigan

1.0
(35)
1.5
(54)
1.2
(43)

0.1
(3)

Chicago

St. Clair & Detroit Rivers
5.3
(187)

0.7
(25)
0.7
(26)
0.7
(26)

Lake Erie

Welland Canal
0.2
(7)

Niagara River
5.8
(205)

0.9
(34)
0.5
(19)
0.4
(14)

Lake Ontario

St. Lawrence River
7.1
(251)

Ottawa River

Mississippi River

Illinois River

Missouri River

Ohio River

Potomac River

Susquehanna River

Delaware River

Legend

Continuously moving weather systems.

Flow through connecting channels.

1. Runoff to lake.
2. Precipitation to lake.
3. Evaporation from lake.

Flow through artificial diversions.

Figures beside arrows represent flow in thousands of cubic metres per second.
Figures in brackets are in thousands of cubic feet per second.
All values are very approximate.
Flow arrows are diagrammatic and not always drawn in strict proportion to the values they represent.

SURFACE RUNOFF

Surface runoff is a major factor in the character of the Great Lakes basin. Rain falling on exposed soil tilled for agriculture or cleared for construction accelerates erosion and the transport of soil particles and pollutants into tributaries. Suspended soil particles in water are deposited as sediment in the lakes and often collect near the mouths of tributaries and connecting channels. Much of the sediment deposited in nearshore areas is resuspended and carried farther into the lake during storms. The finest particles (clays and silts) may remain in suspension long enough to reach the mid-lake areas.

Before settlement of the basin, streams typically ran clear year-round because natural vegetation prevented soil loss. Clearing of the original forest for agriculture and logging has resulted in both erosion and more runoff into the streams and lakes. This accelerated runoff aggravates flooding problems.

GROUNDWATER

Groundwater is important to the Great Lakes ecosystem because it provides a reservoir for storing water and slowly replenishing the lakes in the form of base flow in the tributaries. Shallow groundwater also provides moisture to plants.

As water passes through subsurface areas, some substances are filtered out, but some materials in the soils become dissolved or suspended in the water. Salts and minerals in the soil and bedrock are the source of what is referred to as 'hard' water, a common feature of well water in the lower Great Lakes basin. Groundwater can also pick up man-made materials that have been buried in dumps and landfill sites. Although it is unseen, the underground movement of water is believed to be a major pathway for the transport of pollutants to the Great Lakes. Groundwater may discharge directly to the lakes or indirectly as base flow to the tributaries. Groundwater contamination problems occur in agricultural and urban-industrial areas.

WETLANDS

Wetlands are areas where the water table occurs above the land surface for at least part of the year. When open water is present, it must be less than two metres deep (seven feet), and stagnant or slow moving. Most wetland vegetation emerges and stands erect above the surface.

Four basic types of wetland are encountered in the Great Lakes basin: swamps, marshes, bogs, and fens. Swamps are areas where trees and shrubs live on wet organically rich mineral soils that are flooded for part of the year. Marshes develop in shallow standing water such as ponds and protected bays. Aquatic plants (such as species of rushes) form thick stands which are rooted in the sediment at the bottom of the water, or floating mats where the water is deeper. Swamps and marshes occur most frequently in the southern and eastern portions of the basin.

Bogs form in shallow stagnant water. The most characteristic plant species are the sphagnum mosses which enhance conditions that are too acidic for most other organisms. Dead sphagnum decomposes very slowly accumulating in mats that may eventually become many meters thick and form a dome well above the original surface of the water. It is this material that is excavated and sold as peat moss. Peat also accumulates in fen wetlands. Fens develop in shallow, slowly moving water. They are generally less acidic than bogs. Fens are dominated by sedges and graminoids (grasses), but

Long Point Marshes, Lake Erie.

may include shrubs and stunted trees. Fens and bogs are commonly referred to as peatlands and occur most frequently in the cooler northern and northwestern portions of the Great Lakes basin.

Wetlands are an integral part of the Great Lakes ecosystem because they store water and act as reservoirs, reducing the risk of flooding. They also help to replenish groundwater supplies. Furthermore they can improve the quality of water by filtering sediment, nutrients and contaminants. Some municipalities are beginning to take advantage of this characteristic by using wetlands, especially marshes, as natural sewage treatment systems. Wetland vegetation along lakes and rivers can reduce shoreline erosion by providing a physical buffer between the open water and the shore.

Wetlands also play an important biological role in the ecosystem. They provide habitats for many kinds of plants and animals, some of which are found nowhere else. For ducks, geese and other migratory birds, wetlands are the most important part of the migratory cycle providing food, resting places and seasonal habitats. Wetlands, particularly shoreline and river mouth wetlands, are important spawning and nursery grounds for many species of fish.

LAKE LEVELS

The Great Lakes are part of the global hydrological system. Prevailing westerly winds continuously carry moisture into the basin in air masses from other parts of the continent. At the same time, the basin loses moisture in departing air masses by evaporation and transpiration, and through the outflow of the St. Lawrence River. On average over time, the quantity lost equals what is gained, but lake levels can vary substantially over short-term, seasonal and long-term periods.

Day-to-day changes are caused by winds that push water on shore. This is called 'wind set-up' and is usually associated with a major lake storm which may last for hours or days. Another extreme form of oscillation, known as a seiche, occurs with rapid changes in winds and barometric pressure.

During storms, high winds and rapid changes in barometric pressure cause severe wave conditions at shorelines.

GREAT LAKES HYDROGRAPH. The Hydrograph for the Great Lakes shows the variations in water levels and the relationship of precipitation to water levels.

Annual or seasonal variations in water levels are based mainly on changes in precipitation and runoff to the Great Lakes. Generally the lowest levels occur in winter when much of the precipitation is locked up in ice and snow on land and dry winter air masses pass over the lakes enhancing evaporation. Levels are highest in summer after the spring thaw when runoff increases.

The irregular long-term cycles correspond to long-term trends in precipitation and temperature, the causes of which have yet to be adequately explained. Highest levels occur during periods of abundant precipitation and lower temperatures that decrease evaporation. During periods of high lake levels, storms cause considerable flooding and shoreline erosion which often result in property damage. Much of the damage is attributable to intensive shore development which alters protective dunes and wetlands, removes stabilizing vegetation, and generally reduces the ability of the shoreline to withstand the damaging effects of wind and waves.

The International Joint Commission, the bilateral agency established under the Boundary Waters Treaty of 1909 bet-

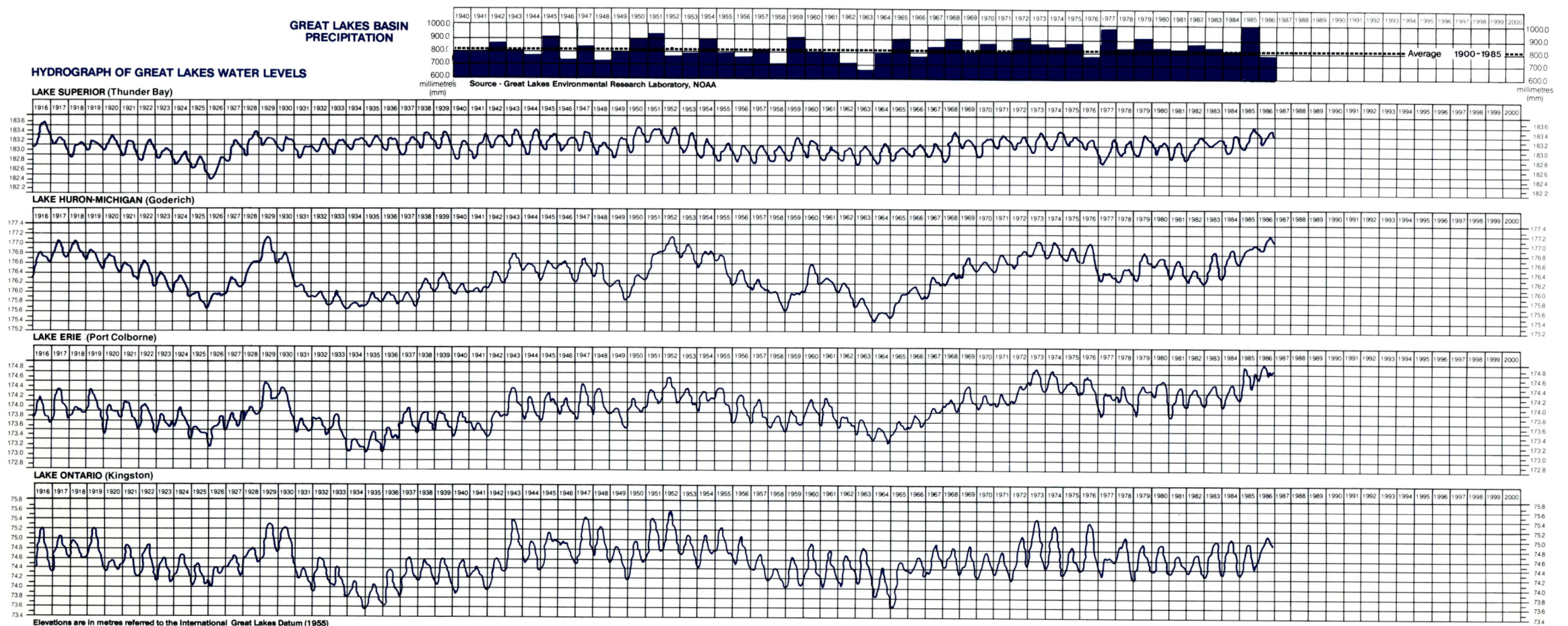

GREAT LAKES BASIN PRECIPITATION

Source - Great Lakes Environmental Research Laboratory, NOAA

Average 1900-1985

HYDROGRAPH OF GREAT LAKES WATER LEVELS

LAKE SUPERIOR (Thunder Bay)

LAKE HURON-MICHIGAN (Goderich)

LAKE ERIE (Port Colborne)

LAKE ONTARIO (Kingston)

Elevations are in metres referred to the International Great Lakes Datum (1955)

ween Canada and the U.S., has the responsibility for limited regulation of flows on the St. Marys and the St. Lawrence rivers. These channels have been altered by enlargement and placement of control works associated with deep-draft shipping. Agreements between the U.S. and Canada govern the flow through the control works on these connecting channels.

The water from Lake Michigan flows to Lake Huron through the Straits of Mackinac. These straits are deep and wide causing lakes Michigan and Huron to stand at the same elevation. There are no artificial controls on the St. Clair and Detroit Rivers which could change the flow from the Michigan-Huron lakes system into Lake Erie. The outflow of Lake Erie via the Niagara River is also uncontrolled, except for some diversion of water through the Welland Canal. A large percentage of the Niagara River flow is diverted through hydroelectric power plants at Niagara Falls, but this diversion has no effect on lake levels.

Studies of possible further regulation of flows and lake levels have concluded that natural fluctuation is huge compared to the influence of existing control works. Further regulation by engineering systems could not be justified in light of the cost and other impacts. Just one inch of water on the surface of lakes Michigan and Huron amounts to more than 36 billion cubic metres of water (about 1260 billion cubic feet).

High Lake levels and severe weather conditions can cause damage to unprotected properties. Right, shoreline damage to the southern shore of Lake Michigan.

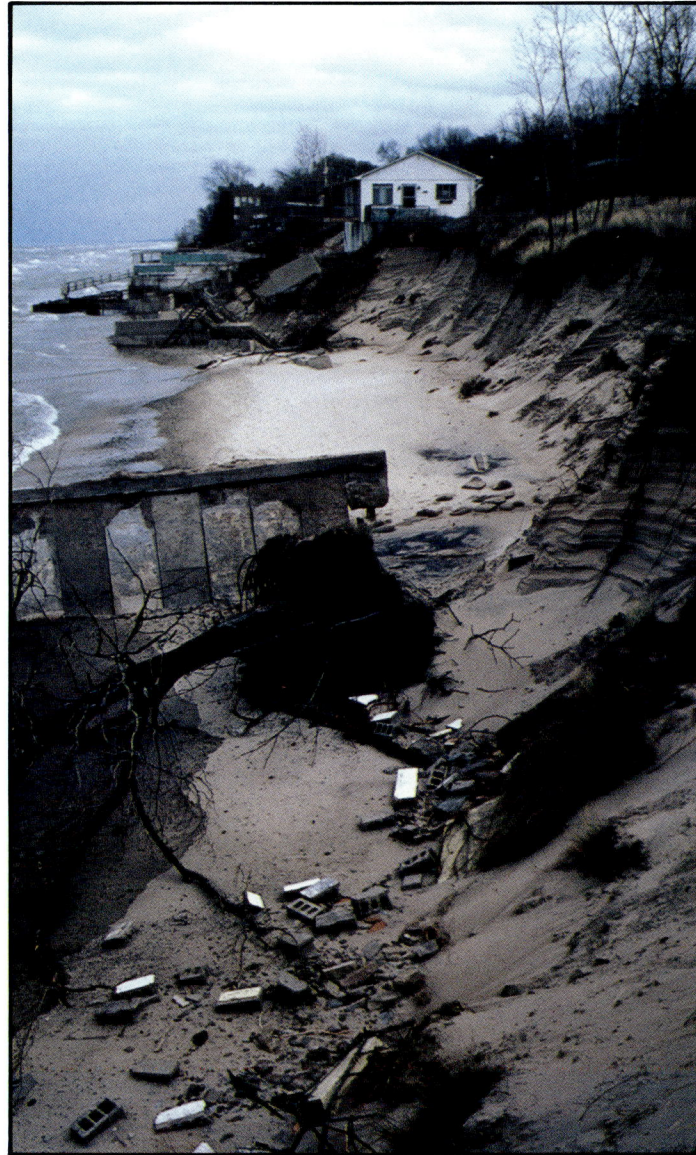

WIND SET-UP is a local rise in water caused by winds pushing water to one side of a lake.

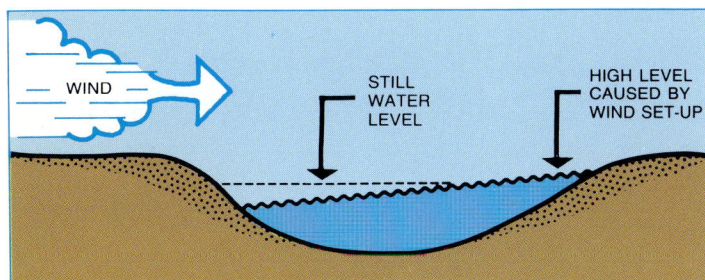

LAKE PROCESSES:
Stratification and Turnover

The Great Lakes are not simply large containers of uniformly mixed water. They are, in fact, highly dynamic systems with complex processes and a variety of subsystems that change seasonally and on longer cycles.

The stratification or layering of water in the lakes is due to density changes caused by changes in temperature. The density of water increases as temperature decreases until it reaches its maximum density at about 4 degrees Celsius (39 degrees Fahrenheit). This causes thermal stratification, or the tendency of deep lakes to form distinct layers in the summer months. Deep water is insulated from the sun and stays

cool and more dense, forming a lower layer called the hypolimnion. Surface and nearshore waters are warmed by the sun, making them less dense so that they form a surface layer called the epilimnion. As the summer progresses, temperature differences increase between the layers. A thin middle layer or thermocline develops in which a rapid transition in temperature occurs.

The warm epilimnion supports most of the life in the lake. Algal production is greatest near the surface where the sun readily penetrates. The surface layer is also rich in oxygen which is mixed into the water from the atmosphere. A second zone of high productivity exists just above the hypolimnion due to upward diffusion of nutrients. The hypolimnion is less productive because it receives less sunlight. In some cases, such as the central basin of Lake Erie, it may lack oxygen due to decomposition of organic matter.

In late fall, surface waters cool, become denser, and descend, displacing deep waters, causing a mixing or turnover of the entire lake. In winter, the temperature of the entire lake approaches four degrees Celsius, while surface waters are cooled to the freezing point and ice can form. As temperatures and densities of deep and shallow waters change with the warming of spring, another turnover may occur. However, in most cases the lakes remain mixed throughout the winter.

Layering of lake water as it warms in summer can prevent the dispersion of effluents from tributaries causing increased concentration of pollutants near the shore.

LAKE STRATIFICATION (Layering) and TURNOVER. Heat from the sun and changing seasons cause water in large lakes to stratify or form layers. In winter, the ice cover stays at 0 degrees C (32 degrees F) and the water remains warmer below the ice than in the air above. Water is most dense at 4 degrees C (39 degrees F). In the spring turnover, warmer water rises as the surface heats up. In fall, surface waters cool, become denser and descend as heat is lost from the surface. In summer, stratification is caused by a warming of surface waters which form a distinct layer called the epilimnion. This is separated from the cooler and denser waters of the hypolimnion by the thermocline, a layer of rapid temperature transition. Turnover distributes oxygen annually throughout most of the lakes.

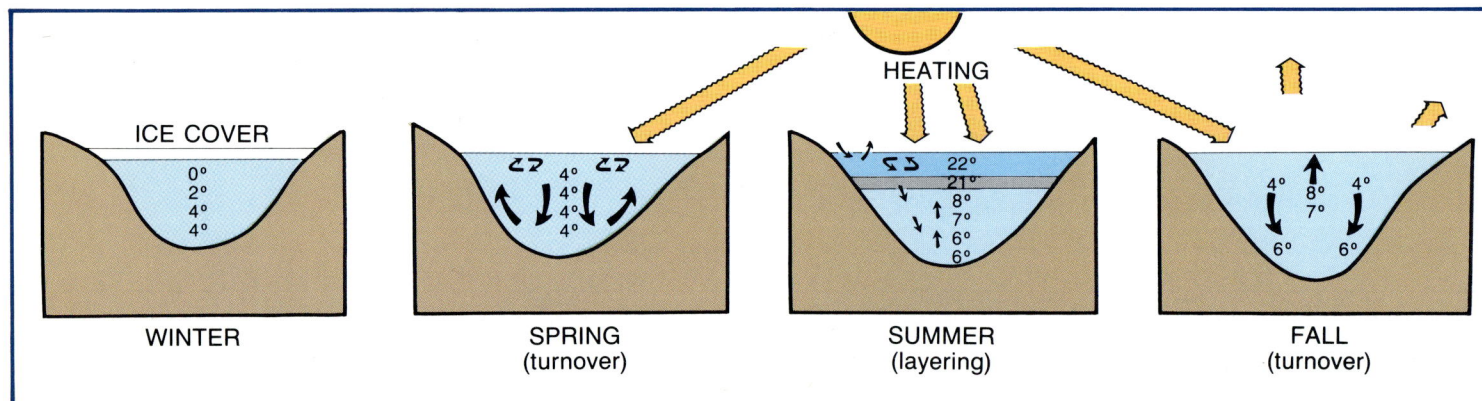

ICE COVER
0°
2°
4°
4°
WINTER

4° 4°
4°
4°
4°
SPRING
(turnover)

HEATING

22°
21°
8°
7°
6°
6°
SUMMER
(layering)

4° 8° 4°
7°
6° 6°
FALL
(turnover)

and nitrogen are present with oxygen, inorganic carbon and adequate water.

Plant material is consumed in the water by zooplankton which graze the waters for algae, and on land by plant-eating animals (herbivores). Next in the chain of energy transfer through the ecosystem are organisms that feed on other animals (carnivores) and those that feed on both animals and plants (omnivores). Together these levels of consumption constitute the food chain, a system of energy transfers through which an ecological community consisting of a complex of species is sustained. The population of each species is determined by a system of checks and balances based on factors such as the availability of food and the presence of predators including disease organisms.

Every ecosystem also includes numerous processes to break down accumulated biomass (plants, animals and their wastes) into the constituent materials and nutrients from which they originated. Decomposition involves micro-organisms that are essential to the ecosystem because they recycle matter which can be used again.

Stable ecosystems are sustained by the interactions that cycle nutrients and energy in a balance between available resources and the life that depends on those resources. In

Double Crested Cormorants and Herring Gulls occupy Big Chicken Island in Lake Erie.

The layering and turnover of water annually are important for water quality. Turnover is the main way in which oxygen-poor water in the deeper areas of the lakes can be mixed with surface water containing more dissolved oxygen. This prevents anoxia or complete oxygen depletion of the lower levels of most of the lakes. However, the process of stratification during the summer also tends to restrict dilution of pollutants from effluents and land runoff.

During the spring warming period, the rapidly warming nearshore waters are inhibited from moving to the open lake by a thermal bar of distinct temperature change that prevents mixing until the sun warms the open lake surface waters or until the waters are mixed by storms. Because the thermal bar holds pollutants nearshore, they are not dispersed to the open waters and can become more concentrated within the nearshore areas at this time.

LIVING RESOURCES

As an ecosystem, the Great Lakes basin is a unit of nature in which living organisms and nonliving things interact adaptively. An ecosystem is fueled by the sun which provides energy in the form of light and heat. This energy warms the earth, the water and the air, causing winds, currents, evaporation and precipitation. The light energy of the sun is essential for the photosynthesis of green plants in water and on land. Plants grow when essential nutrients such as phosphorus

The FOODCHAIN is a simplified way of understanding the process by which organisms in higher trophic levels gain energy by consuming organisms at lower trophic levels. All energy in an ecosystem originates with the sun. The solar energy is transformed by green plants through a process of photosynthesis into stored chemical energy. This is consumed by plant-eating animals which are in turn consumed as food. The concept of the foodchain explains how some persistent contaminants accumulate in an ecosystem and become biologically magnified (see biomagnification and bioaccumulation in Chapter Four).

ecosystems, including the Great Lakes basin, everything depends on everything else and nothing is ever really wasted.

The ecosystem of the Great Lakes and the life supported within it have continuously altered with time. Through periods of climate change and glaciation, species moved in and out of the region, some perished and others pioneered under changed circumstances. None of the changes, however, has been as rapid as that which occurred with the arrival of European settlers.

When the first Europeans arrived in the basin nearly 400 years ago, it was a lush, thickly vegetated area. Vast timber stands, consisting of oaks, maples and other hardwoods dominated the southern areas. Only a very few, small vestiges of the original forest remain today. Between the wooded areas were rich grasslands with growth as high as two or three metres (seven to 10 feet). In the north, coniferous forests occupied the shallow, sandy soils, interspersed by bogs and other wetlands.

The forest and grasslands supported a wide variety of life, such as moose in the wetlands and coniferous woods, and deer in the grasslands and brush forests of the south. The many waterways and wetlands were home to beaver and muskrat which, with the fox, wolf and other fur-bearing species, inhabited the mature forestlands. These were trapped and traded as commodities by the natives and the Europeans. Abundant bird populations thrived on the various terrains, some migrating to the south in winter, others making permanent homes.

It is estimated that there were as many as 180 species of fish native to the Great Lakes. Those inhabiting the near-shore of the lakes included smallmouth and largemouth bass, muskellunge, northern pike and channel catfish. In the open water were lake herring, blue pike, lake whitefish, walleye, sauger, freshwater drum, lake trout and white bass. Because of the differences in the characteristics of the lakes, the species composition varied for each of the Great Lakes. Warm, shallow Lake Erie was the most productive of inshore species, while deep Superior was least productive.

Changes in the species composition of the Great Lakes basin in the last 200 years have been the result of human activities. Many native fish species have been lost by overfishing, habitat destruction or the arrival of exotic or non-native species, such as the lamprey and the alewife. Pollution, especially in the form of nutrient loading and toxic contaminants, has placed additional stresses on fish populations. Other man-made stresses have altered reproductive conditions and habitats, causing some varieties to migrate or perish. Still other effects on lake life result from damming, canal building, altering or polluting tributaries to the lakes in which spawning takes place and where distinct ecosystems once thrived and contributed to the larger basin ecosystem.

Coronelli's 1688 Map of Western New France. The first printed map to show the Great Lakes in their entirety and the most accurate general portrayal of the lakes and tributaries in the 17th century.

CHAPTER THREE

PEOPLE AND THE GREAT LAKES

NATIVE PEOPLE

The first inhabitants of the Great Lakes basin arrived about 10,000 years ago. They had crossed the land bridge from Asia or perhaps had reached South America across the vastness of the Pacific Ocean. Six thousand years ago, descendants of the first settlers were using copper from the south shore of Lake Superior and had established hunting and fishing communities throughout the Great Lakes basin.

The native population in the Great Lakes area is estimated to have been between 60,000 and 117,000 in the 16th century when Europeans began their search for a passage to the Orient through the Great Lakes. The natives occupied widely scattered villages and grew corn, squash, beans and tobac-

co. These were moved once or twice in a generation when the resources in an area became exhausted.

EARLY SETTLEMENT BY EUROPEANS

By the early 1600s, the French had explored the forests around the St. Lawrence Valley and had begun to exploit the area for furs. The first area of the lakes to be visited by Europeans was Georgian Bay, reached via the Ottawa River and Lake Nipissing by the explorer, Samuel de Champlain, or perhaps Etien Brulé, one of Champlain's scouts, in 1615. To the south and east, the Dutch and English began to settle on the eastern seaboard of what is now the United States. Although a confederacy of five Indian nations confined European settlement to the area east of the Appalachians, the

French were able to establish bases in the lower St. Lawrence Valley. This enabled them to penetrate into the heart of the continent via the Ottawa River. In 1670 the French built the first of a chain of Great Lakes forts to protect the fur trade near the Mission of St. Ignace at the Straits of Mackinac. In 1673, Fort Frontenac, on the present site of Kingston, Ontario became the first fort on the lower lakes.

Through the 17th century precious furs were transported to Hochelaga (Montreal) on the Great Lakes routes, but no permanent European settlements were maintained except at forts Frontenac, Michilimackinac and Niagara. After Fort Oswego was established on the south shore of Lake Ontario by the British in 1727, settlement was encouraged in the Mohawk and other valleys leading toward the lakes. A showdown between the British and the French for control of the Great Lakes ended with the British capture of Quebec in 1758.

The British maintained control of the Great Lakes during the American Revolution and, at the close of the conflict, the Great Lakes became the boundary between the new U.S. republic and what remained of British North America. The British granted land to the Loyalists who fled the former New England colonies to Upper and Lower Canada or what are now the southern regions of the provinces of Ontario and Quebec, respectively. Between 1792 and 1800 the population of Upper Canada increased from 20,000 to 60,000. The new American government also moved to develop the Great Lakes region with the passage by Congress of the Ordinance of 1787. This legislation covered everything from land sale to provisions for statehood for the Northwest Territory, the area between the Great Lakes and the Ohio River west of Pennsylvania.

The final military challenge for the wealth of the Great Lakes region came with the War of 1812. For the Americans the war was about the expansion into, and development of, the area around the lakes. For the British, it meant the defense of its remaining imperial holdings in North America. The war proved to be a short one - only two years - but final. When the shooting was over both the Americans and the British claimed victory.

Canada had survived invasion and was set on an inevitable course to nationhood. The new American nation had failed to conquer Upper Canada but gained needed national confidence and prestige. The natives, who had become involved in the war in order to secure a homeland, did not share in the victory. The winners in the War of 1812 were those who dreamed of settling the Great Lakes region. The long-awaited development of the area from a beautiful, almost uninhabited wilderness into a home and workplace for millions began in earnest.

Native peoples were the first to use the many resources of the Great Lakes Basin. Abundant game, fertile soils and plentiful water enabled the early development of hunting, subsistence agriculture and fishing. The lakes and tributaries provided convenient transportation by canoe and trade among groups flourished.

DEVELOPMENT OF THE LAKES

During the next 150 years the development of the Great Lakes basin proceeded with haste. The battles for territory so common during the era of empires and colonies gave way to nation-building, city-building and industrialization. The warriors of the previous era gave way to, or themselves became, the entrepreneurs, farmers and laborers who ran the mills, tilled the soil and provided the skills and services required for modern industrial economies.

The development of the Great Lakes region proceeded along several lines which took advantage of the many resources within the basin. The waterways became major highways of trade and were exploited for their fish. The fertile land that had provided the original wealth of furs and food yielded lumber, then wheat, then other agricultural products. Bulk goods such as iron ore and coal were shipped through Great Lakes ports and manufacturing grew.

AGRICULTURE

The promise of agricultural land was the greatest attraction to the immigrants to the Great Lakes region in the 19th century. By the mid-1800s, most of the Great Lakes region where farming was possible was settled. The population had swelled tremendously. There were about 400,000 people in Michigan, 300,000 in Wisconsin and perhaps half a million in Upper Canada.

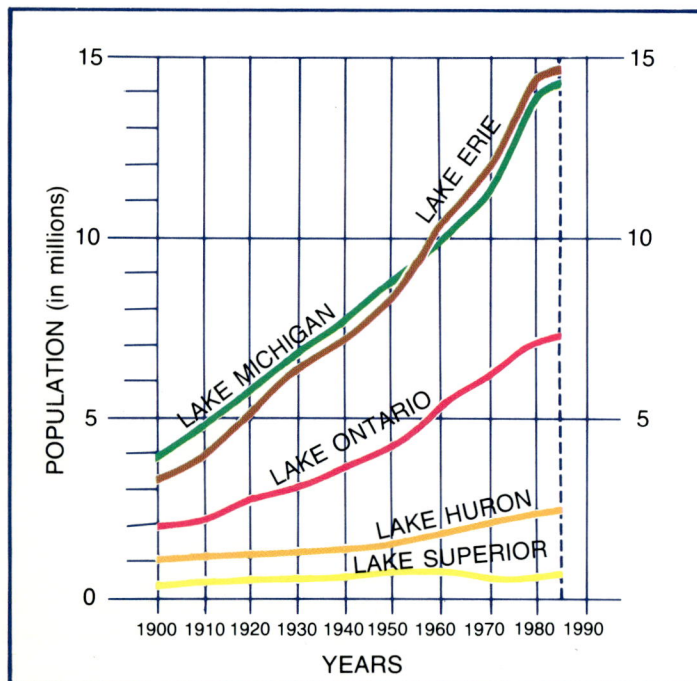

Population Growth in the Great Lakes' Basins Since 1900.

Canals led to broader commodity export opportunities allowing farmers to expand their operations beyond a subsistence level. Wheat and corn were the first commodities to be packed in barrels and shipped abroad. Grist mills - one of the region's first industries - were built on the tributaries flowing into the lakes to process the grains for overseas markets.

As populations grew, dairying and meat production for local consumption began to dominate agriculture in the Great Lakes basin. Specialty crops, such as fruit, vegetables and tobacco, grown for the burgeoning urban population, claimed an increasingly important share of the lands suitable to them.

The rapid, large-scale clearing of land for agriculture brought rapid changes in the ecosystem. Soils stripped of vegetation washed away to the lakes; tributaries and silty deltas clogged and altered the flow of the rivers. Fish habitats and spawning areas were destroyed. Greater surface runoff led to increased seasonal fluctuation in water levels and the creation of more flood-prone lands along the waterway. Agricultural development has also contributed to Great Lakes pollution chiefly in the form of eutrophication. Fertilizers that reach waterways in soils and runoff stimulate growth of algae and other water plants. The plants die and decay, depleting the oxygen in the water. Lack of oxygen leads to fish kills and the character of the ecosystem changes as the original plants and animals give way to more pollution-tolerant species.

Modern row crop monoculture relies heavily on chemicals to control pests such as insects, fungi, and weeds. These chemicals are usually synthetic organic substances and they find their way to rivers and lakes to affect plant and animal life. The problem was first recognized with DDT, a very persistent chemical, which tended to remain in the environment for a long time and to bioaccumulate through the food chain. It caused repoductive failures in some species of birds. Since the use of DDT was banned, some bird populations are now recovering. Other, less persistent, chemicals have replaced DDT and other problem pesticides, but toxic contamination from agricultural practices continues to be a concern. DDT levels in fish are declining but, in spite of being banned, some other pesticides such as dieldrin continue to persist in fish at relatively high levels.

LOGGING AND FORESTRY

The original logging operations in the Great Lakes basin involved clearing the land for agriculture and building houses and barns for the settlers. Much of the wood was simply burned. By the 1830s, however, commercial logging began in Upper Canada. A few years later logging began in Michigan and operations in Minnesota and Wisconsin soon followed.

Once again the lakes played a vital role. Cutting was generally done in the winter months by men from the farms.

Great Lakes Factsheet No. 2
Land and Shoreline Uses

	Superior %	Michigan %	Huron %	Erie %	Ontario %
BASIN LAND USE					
Agricultural					
Canada	0.5		21	80	49
U.S.	6.0	44	40	63	33
Total	3.0	44	27	67	39
Residential					
Canada	0.1		1	4	6
U.S.	3.0	9	6	12	8
Total	1.0	9	2	10	7
Forest					
Canada	98.7		75	15	42
U.S.	80.0	41	52	23	53
Total	91.0	41	68	21	49
Other					
Canada	0.7		3	1	3
U.S.	11.0	6	2	2	6
Total	5.0	6	3	1	5
SHORELINE USE					
Residential					
Canada	n/a		34	39	25
U.S.		39	42	45	40
Recreational					
Canada	n/a		8	8	15
U.S.		24	4	13	12
Agricultural					
Canada	n/a		4	21	30
U.S.		20	15	14	33
Commercial					
Canada	n/a		35	10	18
U.S.		12	32	12	8
Other					
Canada	n/a		19	22	12
U.S.		5	7	16	7

Source: BULLETINS E-1866-70, Sea Grant College Program, Cooperative Extension Service, Michigan State University, E. Lansing, Michigan, 1985.

n/a: not available

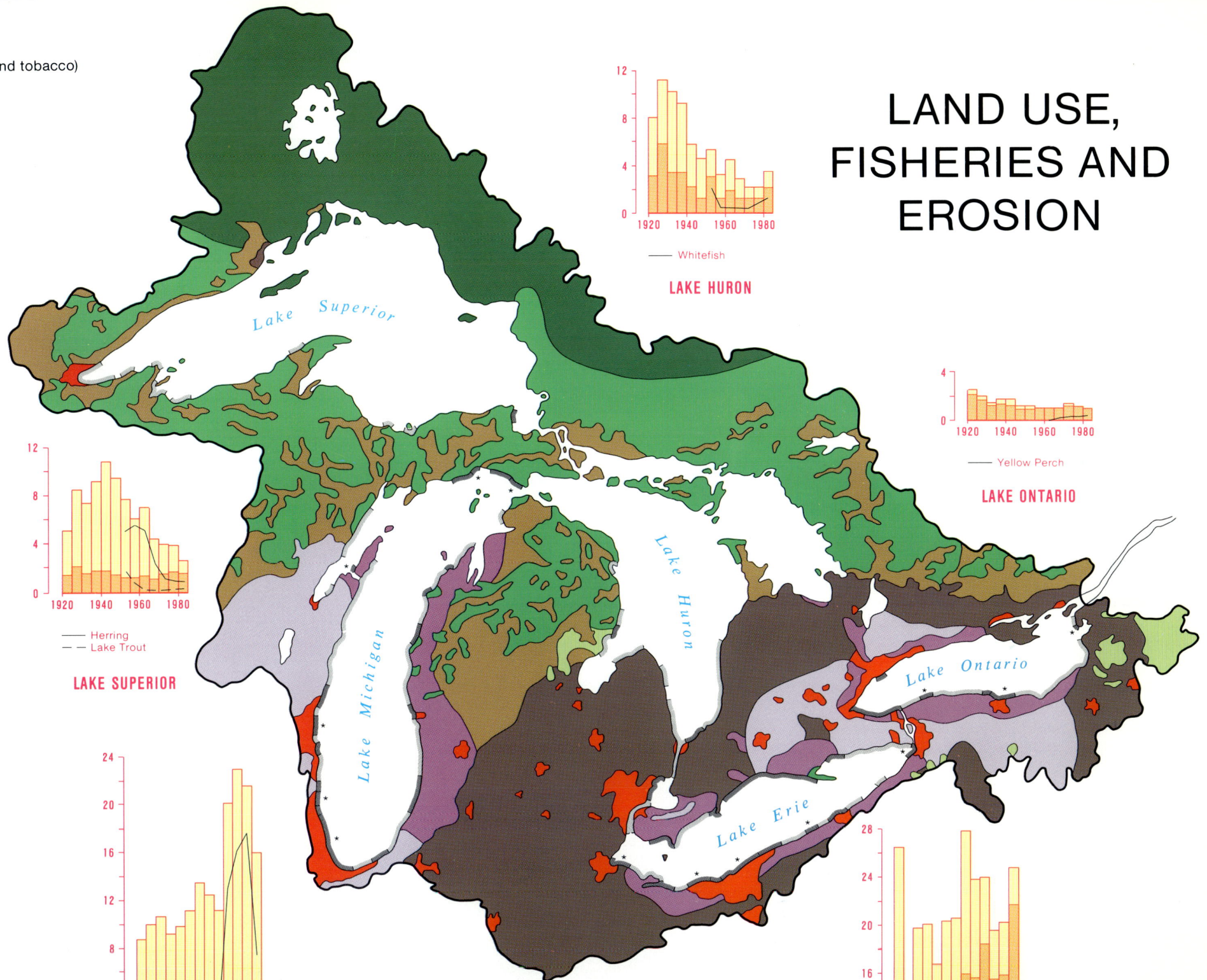

LAND USE, FISHERIES AND EROSION

LAND USE

- Specialized Field Crops (e.g. fruits and tobacco)
- Specialized Dairying
- More Intensive General Farming
- Less Intensive General Farming
- Boreal Forest
- Southeastern Mixed Forest
- Deciduous Forest
- Urban Areas

COMMERCIAL FISHERIES

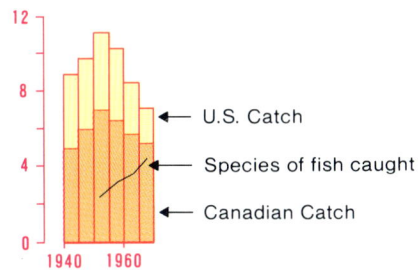

← U.S. Catch

← Species of fish caught

← Canadian Catch

The vertical scale is labelled in units of 1000 tonnes

Tonnes	Tons
4 000	4 400
8 000	8 825
12 000	13 225
16 000	17 625
20 000	22 050
24 000	26 450
28 000	30 875

NOTE:
1. Each bar represents the average catch over a five-year period, except for the last bar which represents four years.
2. Data for individual fish species are not available prior to 1950.
3. The species shown for each lake are those which have been consistently important since 1950. They are not necessarily those which yielded the largest catch in any one five-year period.

SHORELINE EROSION

Minimal

Moderate

Severe

The symbol * denotes shorelines in the United States protected from severe erosion risk by man-made structures. Comparable data is unavailable for Canada.

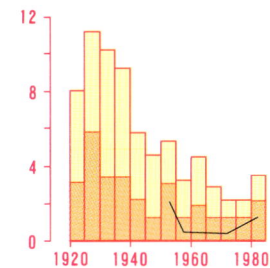

—— Whitefish

LAKE HURON

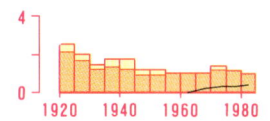

—— Yellow Perch

LAKE ONTARIO

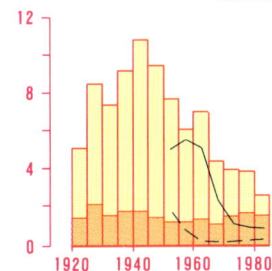

—— Herring
-- Lake Trout

LAKE SUPERIOR

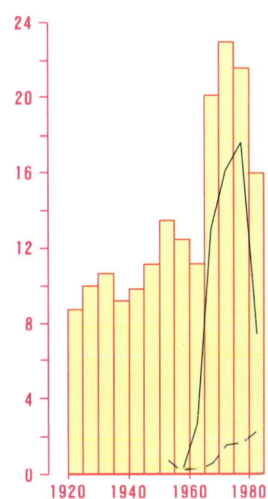

—— Alewife
-- Whitefish

LAKE MICHIGAN

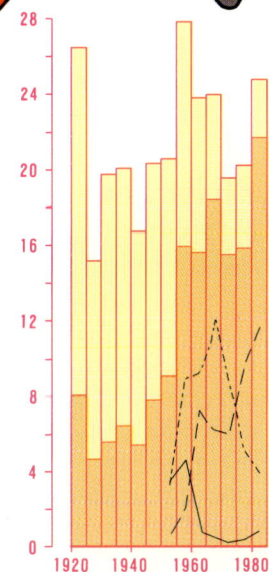

—— Walleye
-- Smelt
-·- Yellow Perch

LAKE ERIE

SCALE 1: 6 000 000

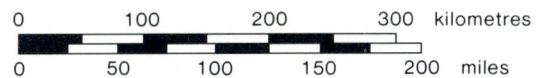

0   100   200   300 kilometres

0   50   100   150   200 miles

Lake Superior

Lake Michigan

Lake Huron

Lake Ontario

Lake Erie

Brock University Cartography

They traveled up the rivers felling trees that were floated down to the lakes during the spring thaw. The logs were formed into huge rafts or loosely gathered in booms to be towed by steam tugs. This latter practice had to be stopped because logs often escaped the boom and seriously interfered with shipping. In time, timber was carried in ships specially designed for log transport.

The earliest loggers mainly harvested white pine. In virgin stands these trees reached 60 metres (200 feet) in height and a single tree could contain 10 cubic metres (6,000 board feet) of lumber. It was light and strong and much in demand for shipbuilding and construction. Each year loggers had to move farther west and north in search of white pine. The trees were hundreds of years old and so were not soon replaced. When the resource was exhausted lumbermen had to utilize other species. The hardwoods such as maple, walnut and oak were cut to make furniture, barrels and specialty products.

Paper-making from pulpwood developed slowly. The first sulphite process paper mill was built on the Welland Canal in the 1860s. Paper production developed at Green Bay in the U.S. and elsewhere in the Great Lakes. Eventually Canada and the U.S. became the world's leading producers of pulp and paper products. Today much of this production still occurs in the Great Lakes area. The pulp and paper industry (along with chloralkali production) contributed to the mercury pollution problem on the Great Lakes until the early 1970s when mercury was banned from use in the industry.

The logging industry was exploitive during its early stages. Huge stands were lost in fires often because of poor management of litter from logging operations. In Canada lumbering was largely done on crown lands with a small tax charged per tree. In the United States cutting was done on private land but when it was cleared the owners often stopped paying taxes and let the land revert to public ownership. In both cases, clearcutting was the usual practice. Without proper rehabilitation of the forest, soils were readily eroded from barren landscapes and lost to local streams, rivers and lakes. In some areas of the Great Lakes basin, however, reforestation has not been adequate and today, as a result, the forests may be a diminishing resource.

CANALS, SHIPPING and TRANSPORTATION

Conflict over the Great Lakes continued after the War of 1812 in the form of competition to improve transportation routes. By 1825 the 364-mile (586 km) Erie Canal, a waterway from Albany, New York to Buffalo, was carrying settlers west and freight east. The cost of goods in the West fell 90 per cent while the price of agricultural products shipped through the lakes rose dramatically. Settlement in the fertile expanses of Ohio and Michigan became even more attractive.

The Canadians opened the Lachine Canal at about the same time to bypass the worst rapids on the St. Lawrence River. In 1829, the Welland Canal joined lakes Erie and Ontario, bypassing Niagara Falls. Other canals linked the Great Lakes to the Ohio and Mississippi Rivers and the Great Lakes became the hub of transportation in eastern North America.

Railroads replaced the canals after mid-century, making still-important transportation links between the Great Lakes and both seacoasts. In 1959, completion of the St. Lawrence Seaway allowed modern ocean vessels to enter the lakes, but shipping has not expanded as much as expected because of intense competition from other modes of transportation such as trucking and railroads.

Today, the three main commodities shipped on the Great Lakes are iron ore, coal and grain. Transport of iron ore has declined as some steel mills in the region have shut down or reduced production, but steel-making capacity in North America is likely to remain concentrated in the Great Lakes region. Coal moves both east and west within the lakes, but coal export abroad has not expanded as much as was anticipated during the rapid rise of oil prices in the 1970s. As a result of economic decline the Great Lakes mid-1980s fleet of over 300 vessels is being reduced through the retirement of the older, smaller vessels.

A Great Lakes freighter passes through the Welland Canal linking lakes Erie and Ontario.

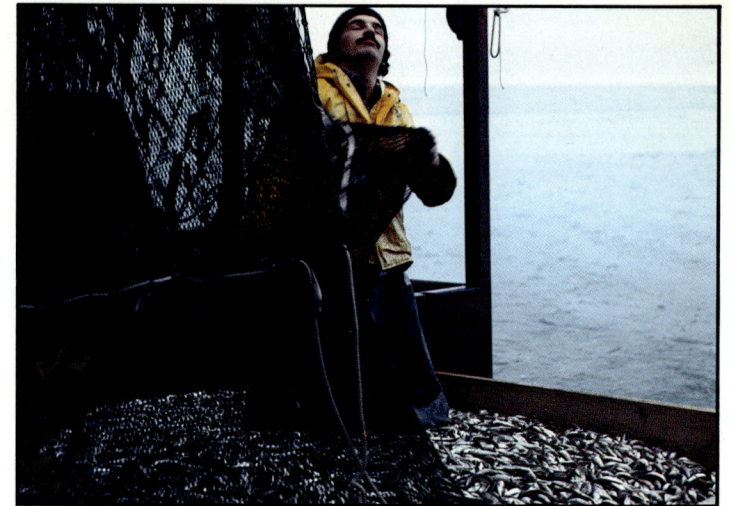

The commercial fishery prospers in a few locations on the lakes. Above, a Lake Erie fisherman out of Port Dover, Ontario harvests a trawl net of smelt.

COMMERCIAL FISHERIES

Fish were important as food for the natives as well as for the first European settlers. Commercial fishing began about 1820 and expanded about 20 per cent per year. The largest Great Lakes fish harvests were recorded in 1889 and 1899 at some 67,000 tonnes (147 million pounds). However, by the 1880s some preferred species in Lake Erie had declined. Catches increased with more efficient fishing equipment but the golden days of the commercial fishery were over by the late 1950s. Since then, average annual catches have been around 50,000 tonnes (110 million pounds). The value of the commercial fishery has declined drastically because the more valuable, larger fish have given way to small and relatively low-value species. Over-fishing, pollution, shoreline and stream habitat destruction, and accidental and deliberate introduction of exotic species such as the sea lamprey all played a part in the decline of the fishery.

Today, lake trout, sturgeon, and lake herring survive in vastly reduced numbers and have been replaced by introduced species such as smelt, alewife, splake, and Pacific salmon. Populations of some of the native species such as yellow perch, walleye and white bass have made good recovery. Lake trout, once the top predator in the lakes, survives in sufficient numbers to allow commercial fishing only in Lake Superior, the only lake where substantial natural reproduction still occurs. However, even in Superior, hatchery reared trout are stocked annually to maintain the population.

Commercial fishing is under continuing pressure from several fronts. Toxic contaminants may force the closure of additional fisheries as the ability to measure the presence of chemicals improves together with the knowledge of their effects on human health.

WATERBORNE COMMERCE

INTER-LAKE COMMODITY FLOW IN TONNES, 1983

Upbound

40 000 000
20 000 000
0

Downbound

Tonnes	Tons
1 000	1 100
100 000	110 250
500 000	453 600
2 500 000	2 755 800
5 000 000	5 511 550
10 000 000	11 025 100
20 000 000	22 046 250
30 000 000	33 069 350
40 000 000	44 092 450

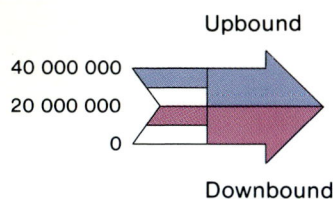

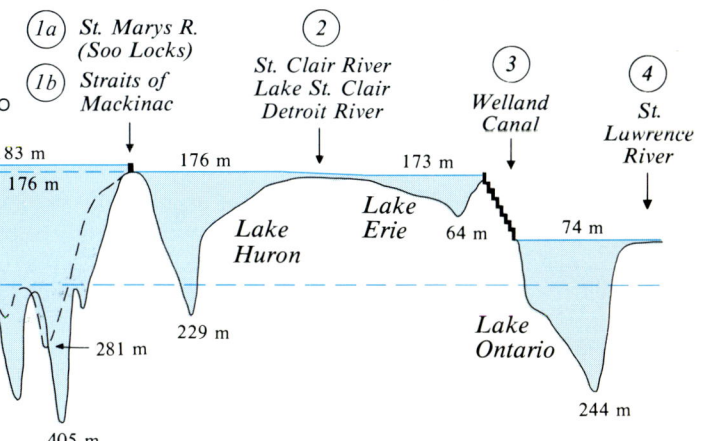

GREAT LAKES PROFILE

1a St. Marys R. (Soo Locks)
1b Straits of Mackinac
2 St. Clair River / Lake St. Clair / Detroit River
3 Welland Canal
4 St. Lawrence River

DULUTH   CHICAGO

Lake Superior
Lake Michigan

SEA LEVEL

183 m
176 m
176 m
Lake Huron
173 m
Lake Erie
64 m
74 m

281 m
229 m
Lake Ontario
405 m
244 m

NOTE:
1. The profile is taken along the long axes of the lakes.
2. The vertical exaggeration is 2 000 times.
3. Lake surface elevations are given above sea level, and maximum depths are below surface level.
4. Inter-lake lock and river systems are numbered to correspond to map.

CARGO VOLUME BY PORT IN TONNES, 1983

PORTS < 2 500 000 TONNES

○ 1 000 - 100 000
○ 100 000 - 500 000
○ 500 000 - 2 500 000

PORTS > 2 500 000 TONNES

● Port Location

Cargo Volume

40 000 000
30 000 000
20 000 000
10 000 000
5 000 000
2 500 000

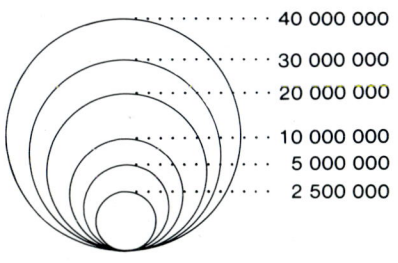

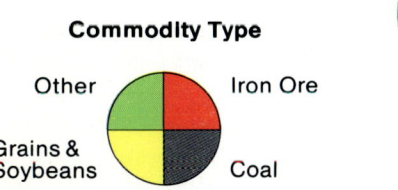

Commodity Type

Other
Iron Ore
Grains & Soybeans
Coal

Commodities in "other" category exceeding 500 000 tonnes or comprising more than 10% of port total

Ce Cement
Ch Chemicals
Co Coke
E Electrical Products
L Limestone
M Metal Products
P Petroleum Products
S Sand and Gravel

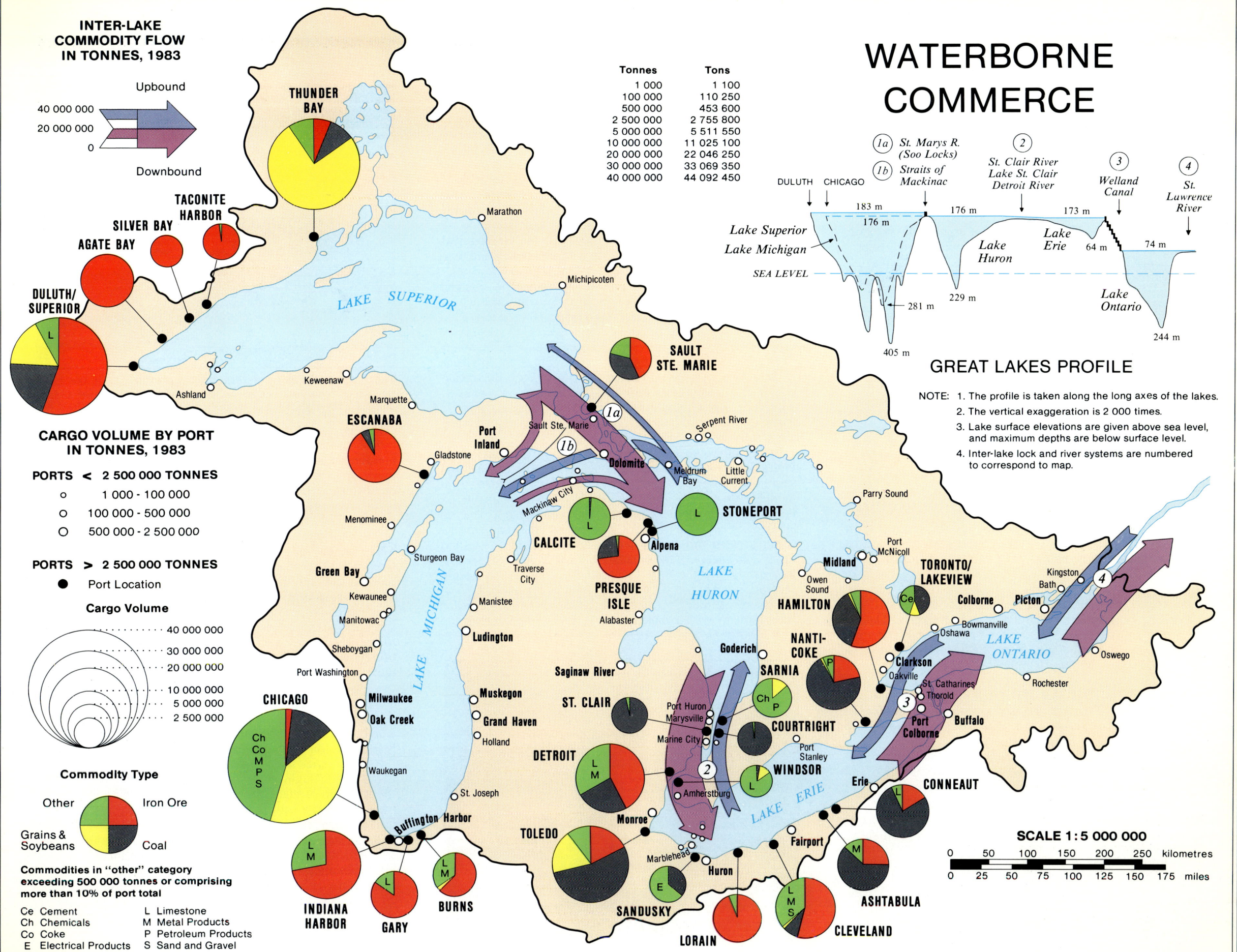

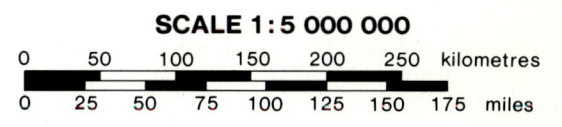

SCALE 1:5 000 000

0 50 100 150 200 250 kilometres
0 25 50 75 100 125 150 175 miles

Map labels

LAKE SUPERIOR
LAKE MICHIGAN
LAKE HURON
LAKE ERIE
LAKE ONTARIO

THUNDER BAY
TACONITE HARBOR
SILVER BAY
AGATE BAY
DULUTH/SUPERIOR
Ashland
Keweenaw
Marquette
Marathon
Michipicoten
Serpent River
SAULT STE. MARIE
ESCANABA
Gladstone
Menominee
Green Bay
Sturgeon Bay
Kewaunee
Manitowac
Sheboygan
Port Washington
CHICAGO
Milwaukee
Oak Creek
Waukegan
INDIANA HARBOR
GARY
BURNS
Buffington Harbor
St. Joseph
Holland
Grand Haven
Muskegon
Manistee
Ludington
Traverse City
Alabaster
Port Inland
Dolomite
Mackinaw City
CALCITE
PRESQUE ISLE
Alpena
STONEPORT
Meldrum Bay
Little Current
Parry Sound
Port McNicoll
Midland
Owen Sound
Goderich
Saginaw River
ST. CLAIR
DETROIT
Port Huron
Marysville
Marine City
Amherstburg
SARNIA
COURTRIGHT
WINDSOR
Port Stanley
NANTICOKE
HAMILTON
TORONTO/LAKEVIEW
Clarkson
Oakville
St. Catharines
Thorold
Port Colborne
Buffalo
Colborne
Bowmanville
Oshawa
Kingston
Bath
Picton
Rochester
Oswego
Erie
CONNEAUT
Fairport
ASHTABULA
CLEVELAND
LORAIN
Huron
Marblehead
SANDUSKY
TOLEDO
Monroe

Brock University Cartography

In addition to the lake trout, lake whitefish, grayling and blue pike of Lake Erie, and the Atlantic salmon of Lake Ontario were the top predators in the open waters of the lakes and were major components of the commercial fishery in earlier times. Of the four, the blue pike, grayling and Lake Ontario salmon are believed to be extinct. The lake whitefish survives in sufficient numbers to support commercial fishing only in Lake Superior and parts of lakes Michigan and Huron. Currently, hatchery-reared coho and chinook salmon are the most plentiful top predators in the open lakes except in the western portion of Lake Erie which is dominated by walleye.

Only pockets remain of the once large commercial fishery. The Canadian commercial fishery in Lake Erie remains prosperous. In 1984, 714 Canadian fishermen harvested a total of about 16,000 tonnes (36.2 million pounds) with a landed value of about $26 million (Canadian). For Canada, the Lake Erie fishery represents nearly two-thirds of the total Great Lakes harvest.

In the United States, the commercial fishery is based on lake whitefish, smelt and perch, and on alewife for animal feed. Commercial fishing is limited by a federal prohibition on the sale of fish affected by toxic contaminants. Pressure to limit commercial fishing in the U.S. is also exerted by sport fishing groups anxious to manage the fishery in their interests. In addition, the trend in the U.S. is to reduce the pressure on the fishery by restricting commercial fishing to trapnets that harvest species selectively, without killing species preferred by recreational fishermen.

SPORT FISHERY

Several factors have contributed to the success of the sport fisheries. The sea lamprey, which almost destroyed the lake trout population, is being successfully controlled using chemical lampricides. Walleye populations rebounded in Lake Erie due to regulation of the commercial fishery and improvements in water quality. The population of alewife exploded as lamprey destroyed native top predators. The increase in alewife provided a forage base for new predators such as coho and chinook salmon which were introduced in the 1960s when lamprey populations declined.

The sport fishery developed quickly as the Pacific salmon rapidly grew to large size after they were introduced into Lake Michigan. Charter fleets developed and a minor tourist boom led to plans to develop a large fish stocking program to fuel a new sport fishing industry.

By 1980, the idea of stocking exotic fish such as salmon to support the sport fishery had spread to all the lakes and jurisdictions. Ontario and Michigan also experimented with the 'splake', a hybrid of the native lake trout and brook (or speckled) trout. None of these predators has been able to reproduce very well if at all, so the fishery has been maintained by stocking year after year. Ironically, the exception is the pink salmon, a small species accidentally introduced to Lake Superior in 1955, that survived to establish spawn-

The development of pleasure boat marinas is one of the recreational activities that has increased in recent years, often placing pressure on the shoreline.

ing populations. They spread through lakes Michigan and Huron, where they established self-propagating populations by the 1980s.

RECREATION

The early explorers and settlers did not come to the Great Lakes region because of opportunities for recreation and leisure activities. Carving out a subsistence economy based on the land and the water resources played a far greater role. However, as the agricultural, industrial and manufacturing economies of the new world developed and matured, the waterways, shorelines and woodlands of the Great Lakes region became attractions to those with the money and time to enjoy the natural wealth.

Recreation in the area became an important economic and social activity with the age of travel in the 19th century. A thriving pleasure-boat industry based on the newly constructed canals developed, bringing people into the region in conjunction with rail and road travel. Niagara Falls attracted travellers from considerable distances and was one of the first stimulants to the growth of a leisure-related economy. Later, the reputation of the lower lakes region as the frontier of a pristine wilderness drew people seeking restful cures and miracle waters to the many spas and 'clinics' which developed along the waterway.

In the 20th century, more people had more free time. With industrial growth, greater personal disposable income and shorter work weeks, people of all walks of life began to spend their leisure time beyond the city limits. Governments on both sides of the border acquired lands and began to develop an extensive system of parks, wilderness areas and conservation areas in order to protect valuable local resources and to serve the needs of the population for recreation areas. Unfortunately, by the time the need for publicly accessible recreation lands had become apparent, much of the land in the basin, including virtually all the shoreline on the lower lakes, was in private hands. Today, about 80 percent of the U.S. shoreline and 20 percent of the Canadian shore is

The sandy beaches of the lower lakes provide one of the most popular summer recreational activities on the lakes. Above, the Indiana Dunes National Lakeshore on Lake Michigan.

privately owned and not accessible to the public.

The recreation industry includes sport outfitters, boat builders, marinas, resorts and restaurants. The economy of many areas within the basin relies heavily on tourism and the revenues from local recreational activities nearby. In some areas, recreation and tourism are actively being sought to replace losses resulting from economic decline in manufacturing.

The increasingly intensive recreational development of the Great Lakes has had mixed results. On the one hand many recreational activities cause environmental damage. Extensive development of cottage areas, summer home sites, beaches and marinas has resulted in land clearance and shoreline alteration. The removal of vegetation and changes to beaches, dune structures and other natural shore protection have stepped up erosion in some areas. Effluent from recreational sites has generally not been as well treated as sewage from cities, posing local water quality problems such as enrichment and bacterial contamination. Also, increased development in areas susceptible to natural flooding and erosion has increased pressure to manage lake levels to protect real estate that was unwisely developed.

On the other hand greater recreational use of the Great Lakes has brought environmental problems in the lakes to the attention of many more people. Environmental damage often interferes with recreational uses. Hence, people who use the water for its fun and beauty can become a potent force in the protection of the ecosystem. Naturalists, anglers and cottagers were among the first to bring environmental issues to the attention of the public and call for the cleanup of the lakes in the 1950s and 1960s when eutrophication threatened favored fishing, bathing and wildlife sites. Today more people than ever use and value the lakes for recreational purposes.

RECREATION AND SPORTS

PROTECTED AREAS

- National Park
- Provincial/State Park
- National Forest
- State Forest
- National Lakeshore
- National Wildlife Area/Refuge
- National Recreation Area
- Underwater Preserve

RECREATIONAL AREAS AND ROUTES

- ▲ Ski Area
- Canalized Waterway
- Canoe Route
- Long-distance Trail

Not all sections of the trails shown are yet in existence.

SPORT FISHING

- Other
- Salmon and Steelhead Trout
- Perch
- Lake Trout and other Trout
- Bass and White Bass
- Walleye, Sauger, Pike, Pickerel and Muskie

NOTE:
1. Circle areas are proportional to the number of angler days in 1983: Lake Superior - 2 576 000, Lake Michigan - 27 170 000, Lake Huron - 18 667 000, Lake Erie - 43 409 000, and Lake Ontario - 18 519 000.
2. The data measures sport fishing effort, and is classified according to species sought as opposed to species actually caught.
3. Significant species in the "other" category are: C - catfish and bullhead, P - panfish, and S - sheephead.
4. The "other" category also includes those cases where the angler has no preference for the species caught.

RECREATIONAL BOATING FACILITIES

- Sparse
- Moderate
- Dense

SPECTATOR SPORTS

- Hockey
- Baseball
- Football
- Basketball
- Major League
- Minor League

NOTE:
1. The leagues represented are as follows:
   Baseball: American League, National League and Triple A
   Basketball: National Basketball Association and Division One Colleges
   Football: National Football League, Canadian Football League and Division One Colleges
   Hockey: National Hockey League, American Hockey League, International Hockey League and Ontario League
2. The minor leagues are selected on the basis of level of play and spectator attendance.
3. Where a sport has major and minor league teams in the same location only the major league team is shown.
4. Where a sport has more than one major or minor league team in the same location only one is shown.

SCALE 1:5 000 000

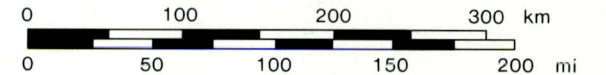

0 100 200 300 km
0 50 100 150 200 mi

Map labels

LAKE SUPERIOR
LAKE MICHIGAN
LAKE HURON
LAKE ONTARIO
LAKE ERIE

Isle Royale National Park
Pukaskwa National Park
Superior National Forest
Chequamegon National Forest
Ottawa National Forest
Nicolet National Forest
Hiawatha National Forest
Manistee National Forest
Huron National Forest
Bruce Peninsula National Park
Georgian Bay Islands National Park
Point Pelee National Park

Voyageur Trail
North Country National Scenic Trail
Michigan's Shore to Shore Trail
Buckeye Trail
Bruce Trail
Hiking Trail
Ganaraska Trail
Rideau Trail
Finger Lakes Trail
Trent-Severn Waterway
Rideau Canal
Inland Waterway
Welland Canal
New York State Barge Canal
Erie Barge Canal
Barge Canal Recreationway

Sault Ste. Marie
Sudbury
North Bay
Peterborough
Belleville
Kingston
Newmarket
Oshawa
Toronto
Rochester
Guelph
Kitchener
Niagara Falls
Hamilton
London
Buffalo
Syracuse
Ithica
Green Bay
Milwaukee
Muskegon
Evanston
Chicago
Valparaiso
Fort Wayne
Kalamazoo
Mount Pleasant
Saginaw
Flint
Lansing
Ann Arbor
Ypsilanti
Detroit
Windsor
Toledo
Bowling Green
Cleveland

Brock University Cartography

URBANIZATION and INDUSTRIAL GROWTH

Nearly all the settlements that grew into cities in the Great Lakes region were established on the waterways that transported people, raw materials and goods. The largest urban areas developed at the mouths of tributaries due to transportation advantages and the apparently inexhaustible supply of fresh water for domestic and industrial use. Historically, the major industries in the Great Lakes region have produced steel, paper, chemicals, automobiles and other manufactured goods.

A large part of the steel industry in Canada and the United States is concentrated in the Great Lakes because iron ore, coal and limestone can be carried on the lakes from mines and quarries to steel mills. In the United States, ore is carried from mines near Lake Superior to steel mills at the south end of Lake Michigan and at Detroit, Cleveland, and Lorain in the Lake Erie basin. In Canada, ore from the upper lakes region is processed in steel mills at Sault Ste. Marie, Hamilton and Nanticoke.

Paper-making in the U.S. occurs primarily on the upper lakes, with the largest concentration of mills along the Fox River that feeds into Green Bay on Lake Michigan. In Canada, mills are located along the Welland Canal as well as along the upper lakes. Chemical industries developed on both sides of the Niagara River because of the availability of cheap electricity. Other major concentrations of chemical production are located near Saginaw Bay in Lake Huron and in Sarnia, Ontario on the St. Clair River, because of abundant salt deposits and plentiful water.

All of these industrial activities produce vast quantities of wastes. Initially the wastes of urban-industrial centers did

The City of Chicago on Lake Michigan is the largest urban area on the lakes.

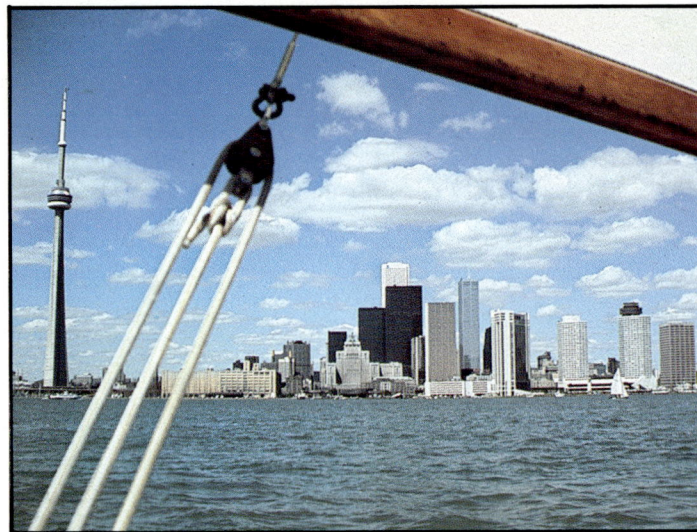

The City of Toronto on Lake Ontario is the largest Canadian city on the lakes.

not appear to pose serious problems. Throughout most of the 19th century industrial wastes were dumped into the waterways, diluted and dispersed. Eventually, problems emerged when municipal water supplies became contaminated with urban-industrial effluent. The threat to public health from disease organisms prompted some cities to adopt practices that seemed for the time to solve the problem.

In 1854, Chicago experienced a cholera epidemic in which five percent of the population perished, and in 1891, the rate of death due to typhoid had reached a high of 124 per 100,000 population. To protect its drinking water supply from sewage, Chicago reversed the flow of the Chicago River away from Lake Michigan. A diversion channel was dug to carry sewage effluent away from Lake Michigan into the Illinois and Mississippi River system. In Hamilton, in the 1870s, water could no longer be drawn from the harbor or from local wells because of contamination. A steam powered water pump was installed to draw deep water from Lake Ontario for distribution throughout the city.

Many of the dangers of industrial pollution to the Great Lakes and to human and environmental health were not recognized until recently, in part because their presence and their effects are difficult to detect. In recent years this has become especially evident where aging industrial disposal sites leak chemicals discarded many years ago into the environment or where sediments contaminated by long-standing industrial activities continue to contribute dangerous pollutants to the waterways. Now the region must cope with cleanup of the pollution from these past activities at the same time that the industrial base for the regional economy is struggling to remain competitive.

Use of Great Lakes resources brought wealth and well-being to the residents of Great Lakes cities but the full price of the concentration of industry and people is only now be-

ing understood. The cleanup of the Great Lakes region will require continuous expenditure by, and cooperation among state, provincial and federal agencies, local governments and industry.

MAJOR DIVERSION PROPOSALS

A number of proposals have been made for large-scale diversion of water from water-rich regions of North America to water-poor areas experiencing growth in population and industry. The plans generally call for interbasin transfer of Great Lakes water or Canada's Arctic waters southward to the western U.S. Massive engineering schemes needed to do this have often been proposed by private entrepreneurs interested in selling the water or benefitting from improved water supply to their area.

In the 1960s, a California engineering firm proposed a "North American Water and Power Alliance" (NAWAPA). The plan included diversion of water from Alaska and northwestern Canada through a major valley in the Canadian Rockies (Rocky Mountain Trench) for distribution as far as Mexico by a system of canals and rivers. Efforts to revive NAWAPA in the 1970s failed.

At the direction of the U.S. Congress the U.S. Army Corps of Engineers studied the possibility of diversion of water from the Great Lakes via the Mississippi River to compensate for rapid depletion of groundwater from the Ogallala aquifer in the high plains states of Nebraska, Kansas, Oklahoma and Texas. A Colorado proposal called for a canal or a pipeline to carry water from the Great Lakes to rapidly growing economies in the Southwest. Both ideas were opposed by all Great Lakes states and the Province of Ontario.

The Great Recycling and Northern Development (GRAND) Canal concept was revived in 1985 after being proposed in the 1950s. The plan calls for turning James Bay into a freshwater lake using a dam to prevent mixing with saltwater from Hudson Bay. Fresh water would then be pumped over the Arctic divide and transferred into the Great Lakes. Great Lakes water would in turn be diverted for sale to western states. Development would require an estimated $100 billion and the support of Ontario and all the Great Lakes states as well as the federal governments of both countries.

Invariably the proposals have failed to materialize for economic reasons. Increasingly, however, opposition to these proposals is based on environmental concerns because the environmental impacts of large-scale diversions have not been adequately assessed. In the 1985 Great Lakes Charter all the state governors and the premiers of Ontario and Quebec agreed to cooperate in consideration of any proposed diversion.

EMPLOYMENT AND INDUSTRIAL STRUCTURE

SCALE 1: 7 500 000

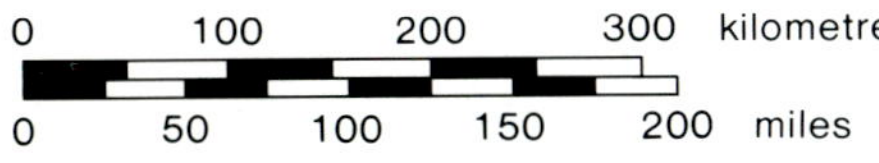

0   100   200   300 kilometres
0   50   100   150   200 miles

POPULATION AND EMPLOYMENT, 1980 (USA), 1981 (CANADA)

NUMBER OF PEOPLE

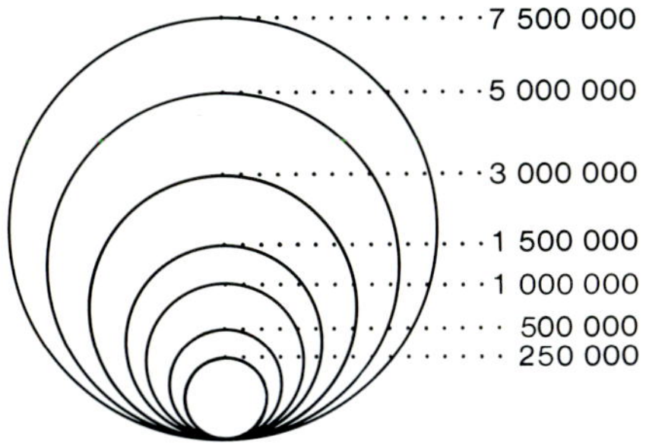

- 7 500 000
- 5 000 000
- 3 000 000
- 1 500 000
- 1 000 000
- 500 000
- 250 000

EMPLOYMENT BREAKDOWN

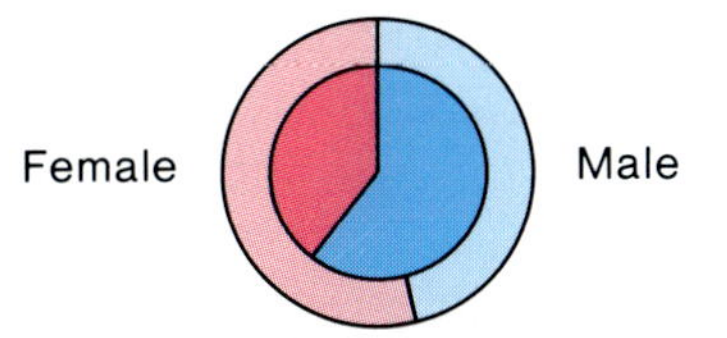

Female   Male

Outer circle - total population
Inner circle - working population

INDUSTRIAL STRUCTURE, 1980 (USA), 1981 (CANADA)

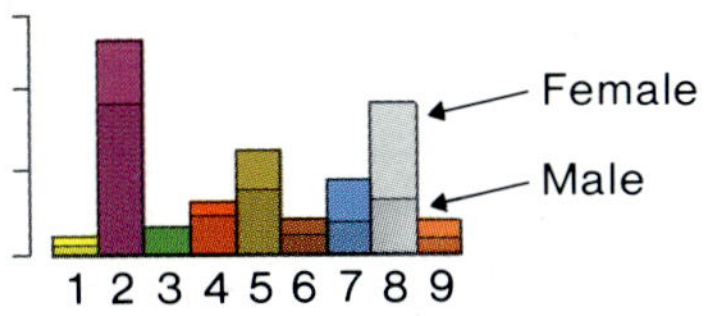

Female
Male

1 2 3 4 5 6 7 8 9

The vertical scale is labelled in units of 100 000 people.

1. Primary industry (agriculture, forestry, mining, etc.)
2. Manufacturing
3. Construction
4. Transportation and communications
5. Trade (retail and wholesale)
6. Finance, insurance, and real estate
7. Personal services (recreation, repairs, hotels, etc.)
8. Community services (health, education, religion, etc.)
9. Public administration and defence

Graphs of Industrial Structure are shown only for statistical areas with populations exceeding 750 000.

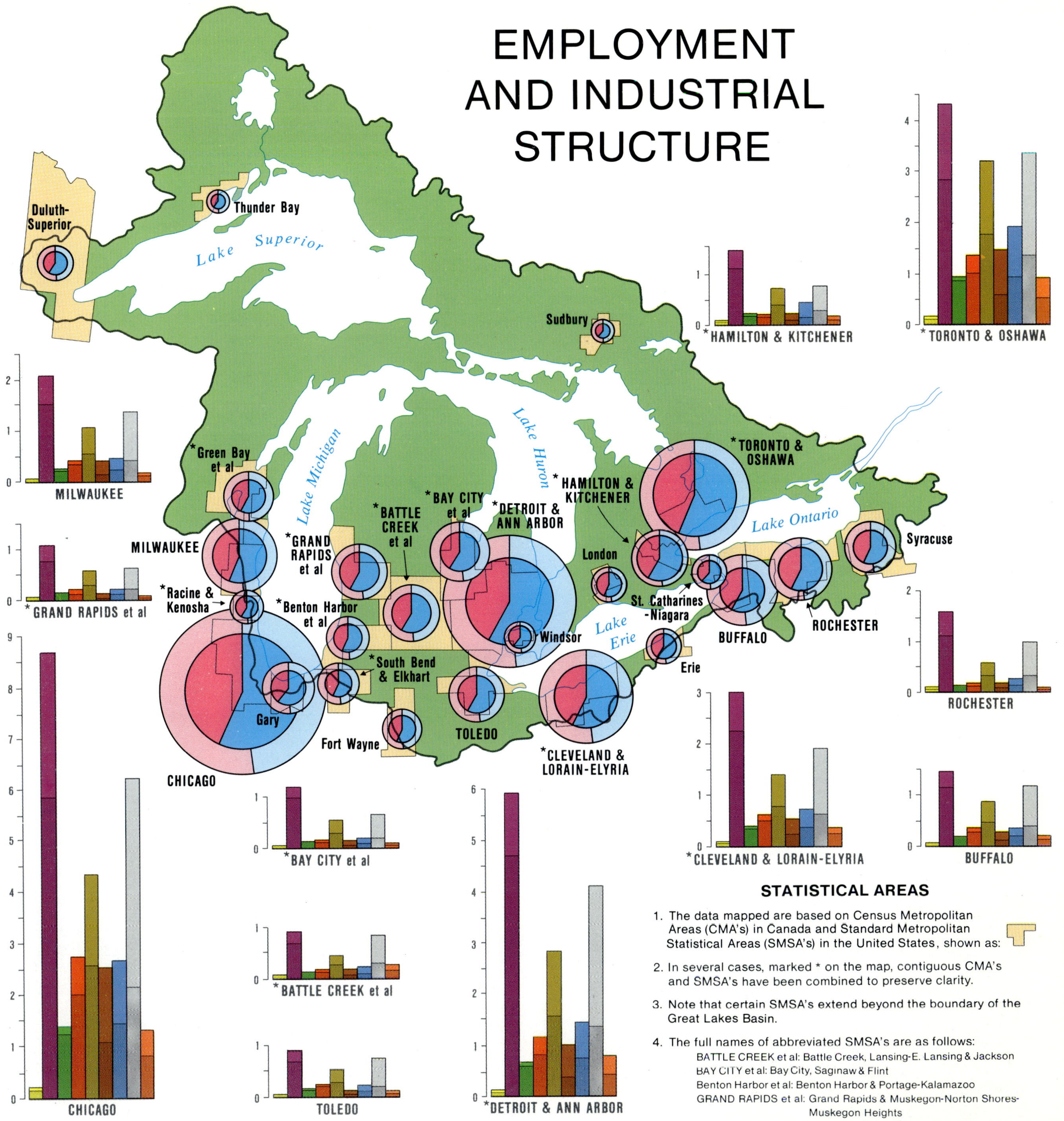

STATISTICAL AREAS

1. The data mapped are based on Census Metropolitan Areas (CMA's) in Canada and Standard Metropolitan Statistical Areas (SMSA's) in the United States, shown as:

2. In several cases, marked * on the map, contiguous CMA's and SMSA's have been combined to preserve clarity.

3. Note that certain SMSA's extend beyond the boundary of the Great Lakes Basin.

4. The full names of abbreviated SMSA's are as follows:
   BATTLE CREEK et al: Battle Creek, Lansing-E. Lansing & Jackson
   BAY CITY et al: Bay City, Saginaw & Flint
   Benton Harbor et al: Benton Harbor & Portage-Kalamazoo
   GRAND RAPIDS et al: Grand Rapids & Muskegon-Norton Shores-Muskegon Heights
   Green Bay et al: Green Bay, Sheboygan & Appleton-Oshkosh

Map labels

Lake Superior
Lake Michigan
Lake Huron
Lake Ontario
Lake Erie

Duluth-Superior
Thunder Bay
Sudbury
*Green Bay et al
*GRAND RAPIDS et al
MILWAUKEE
*Racine & Kenosha
*Benton Harbor et al
*BATTLE CREEK et al
*BAY CITY et al
*DETROIT & ANN ARBOR
HAMILTON & KITCHENER
London
*TORONTO & OSHAWA
St. Catharines -Niagara
Windsor
Syracuse
ROCHESTER
BUFFALO
Erie
*South Bend & Elkhart
Gary
Fort Wayne
CHICAGO
TOLEDO
*CLEVELAND & LORAIN-ELYRIA

Bar chart labels

*HAMILTON & KITCHENER
*TORONTO & OSHAWA
MILWAUKEE
*GRAND RAPIDS et al
*BAY CITY et al
*BATTLE CREEK et al
CHICAGO
TOLEDO
*DETROIT & ANN ARBOR
*CLEVELAND & LORAIN-ELYRIA
ROCHESTER
BUFFALO

Brock University Cartography

ROADS AND AIRPORTS

AIRPORTS
- ✳ Major
- ● Minor

ROADS
- ▬ Toll Road
- ▬ Other Limited Access Road
- ▬ Trans Canada Highway
- ▬ Other Main Road
- ╌ Ferry Service

Thunder Bay
Duluth
Lake Superior
Sault Ste. Marie
Sudbury
North Bay
Lake Michigan
Lake Huron
TORONTO
Lake Ontario
Rochester
Syracuse
Milwaukee
Grand Rapids
Flint
Hamilton
London
Buffalo
Lansing
DETROIT
Lake Erie
CHICAGO
Toledo
Fort Wayne
Cleveland

PIPELINES

PIPELINES
- ▬ Oil
- ▬ Gas

Thunder Bay
Duluth
Lake Superior
Sault Ste. Marie
Sudbury
North Bay
Lake Michigan
Lake Huron
TORONTO
Lake Ontario
Rochester
Syracuse
Milwaukee
Grand Rapids
Flint
Hamilton
London
Buffalo
Lansing
DETROIT
Lake Erie
Toledo
Cleveland
Fort Wayne

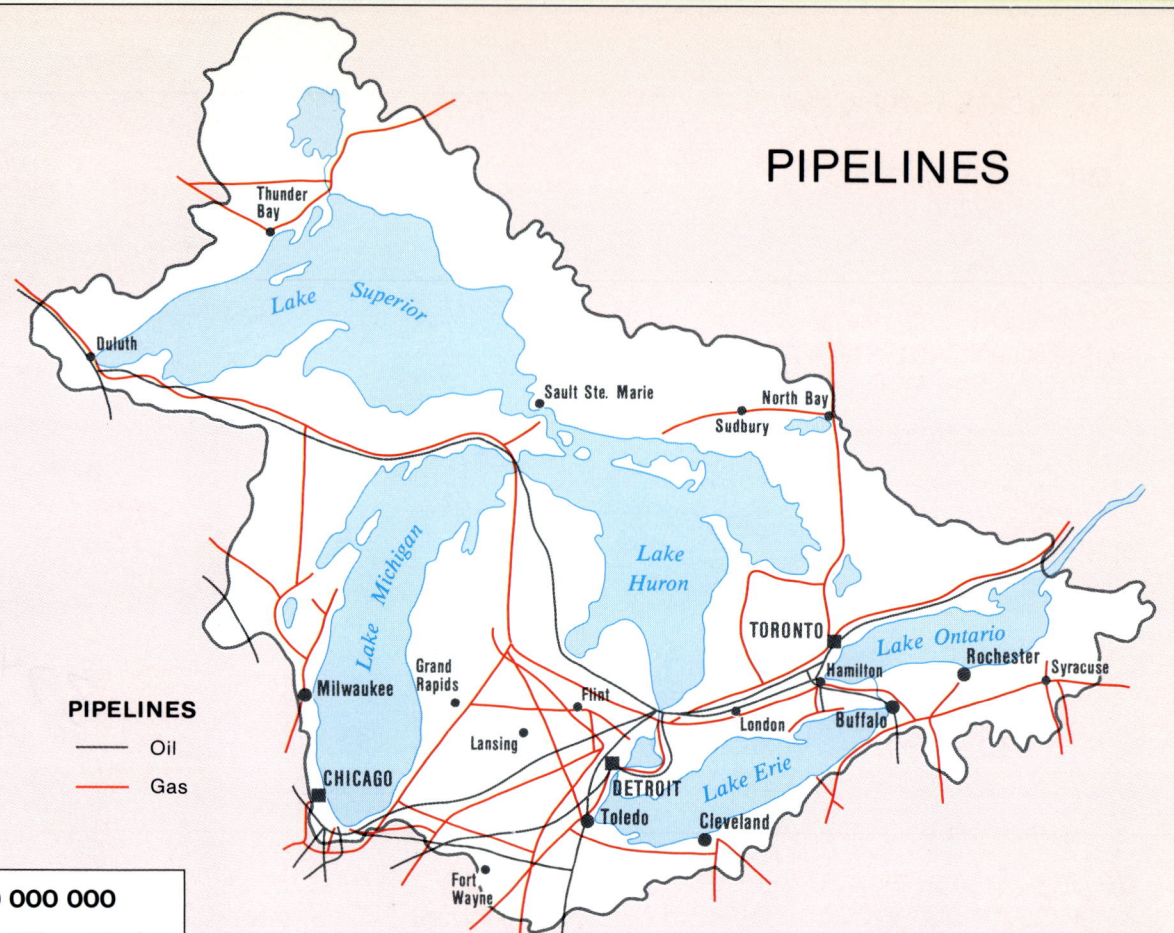

SCALE 1:10 000 000

0 100 200 300 400 km

0 50 100 150 200 250 mi

RAILROADS

RAILROADS
- ▬ Passenger and Freight Lines
- ▬ Freight Line
- ╌ Ferry Service

Thunder Bay
Duluth
Lake Superior
Sault Ste. Marie
Sudbury
North Bay
Lake Michigan
Lake Huron
TORONTO
Lake Ontario
Rochester
Syracuse
Milwaukee
Grand Rapids
Flint
Hamilton
London
Buffalo
Lansing
DETROIT
Lake Erie
CHICAGO
Toledo
Cleveland
Fort Wayne

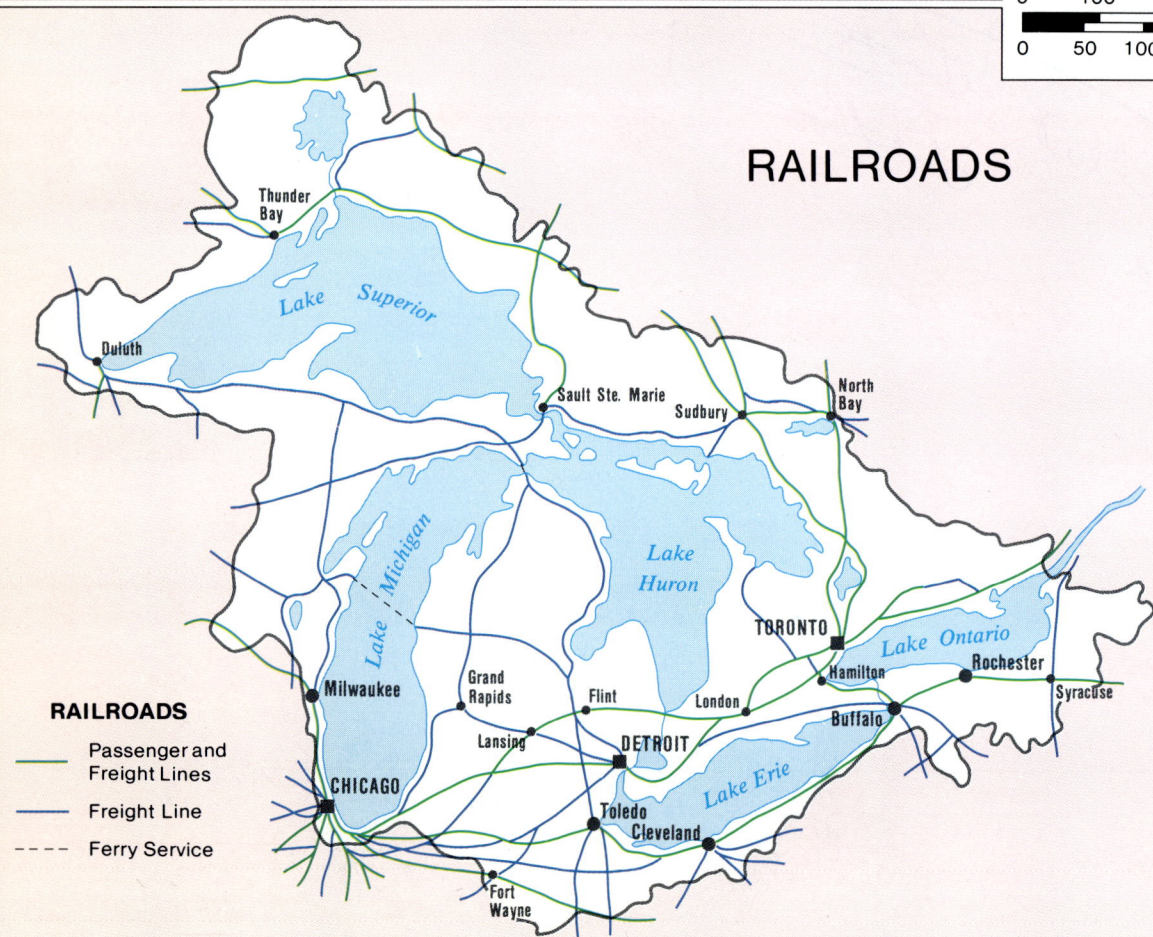

ELECTRICAL POWER LINES AND GENERATING STATIONS

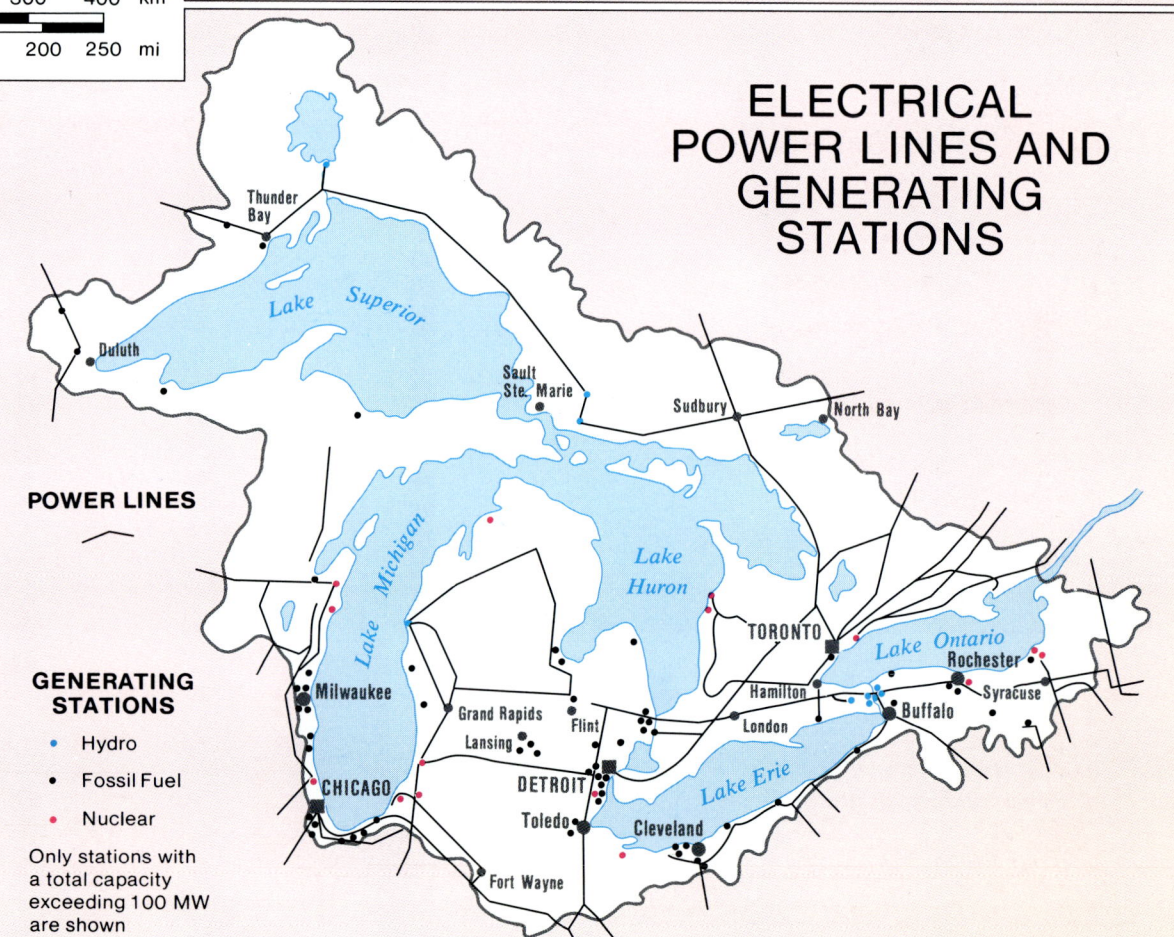

POWER LINES
▬

GENERATING STATIONS
- ● Hydro
- ● Fossil Fuel
- ● Nuclear

Only stations with a total capacity exceeding 100 MW are shown

Thunder Bay
Duluth
Lake Superior
Sault Ste. Marie
Sudbury
North Bay
Lake Michigan
Lake Huron
TORONTO
Lake Ontario
Rochester
Syracuse
Milwaukee
Grand Rapids
Flint
Hamilton
London
Buffalo
Lansing
DETROIT
Lake Erie
CHICAGO
Toledo
Cleveland
Fort Wayne

LEVELS, DIVERSIONS and CONSUMPTIVE USE STUDIES

The responsibilities of the International Joint Commission (IJC) for levels and flows of the Great Lakes are separate from its responsibilities for water quality. Water quality objectives are set by the Great Lakes Water Quality Agreement but levels and flows decisions are made to comply with the terms of the 1909 Boundary Waters Treaty.

Only limited controls of levels and flows are possible and only for Lake Superior and Lake Ontario. The flows are controlled by locks and dams on the St. Marys River, at Niagara Falls and in the St. Lawrence. Special boards of experts advise the IJC how to meet the terms of the treaty. Members of the binational control boards are equally divided between government agencies in both countries. Until 1973, the IJC managed levels and flows for navigation and hydropower production purposes. Since then, the IJC has tried to balance these interests with prevention of shore erosion.

The IJC has carried out several special studies on levels issues in response to references, or requests, from the governments. In 1964, when water levels were very low, the governments asked the IJC whether it would be feasible to maintain the waters of all the Great Lakes, including Michigan and Huron, at a more constant level. After a nine year study, in 1973, when water levels were very high, the IJC advised the governments that the high costs of an engineering system for further regulation of Michigan and Huron could not be justified by the benefits.

The same conclusion was reached for further regulation of Lake Erie in 1983. With water levels even higher in 1986, many shore property owners who disagree with the conclusions of the earlier studies are urging the governments to reduce water levels by increased diversions regardless of costs.

Diversion means transfer of water from one watershed to another. In 1982 the IJC reported on a study of the effects of existing diversions into and out of the Great Lakes system and on consumptive uses. "Diversion" means transfer of water from one watershed to another. "Consumptive use" measures the difference between the amount of water that is withdrawn and the amount that is returned to the waterway after use.

At present, water is diverted into the Great Lakes system from the Hudson Bay watershed through Long Lac and Lake Ogoki and diverted out of the Great Lakes at Chicago. These diversions are almost equally balanced and have had little long term effect on levels of the lakes. The study concluded that climate and weather changes affect levels of the lakes far more than existing man-made diversions.

Most consumptive use in the Great Lakes is due to evaporation from power plant cooling systems. Until this study, consumptive use had not been considered significant for the Great Lakes because the volume of water in the system is so large. The 1983 report concluded that, if consumptive use of water continues to increase, outflows through the St. Lawrence River could be reduced by as much as eight per cent by around the year 2030.

Levels of all the Great Lakes have been relatively high since the early 1970s. They are expected to remain high if the trend toward wetter, colder weather continues in the region. Shore property owners concerned about erosion are urging that diversions be increased. Consequently the IJC may receive a new reference from the governments on diversions. A reference on lake levels was received in 1985.

Great Lakes Factsheet No. 3A
Water Withdrawals

	Superior	Michigan	Huron	Erie	Ontario	TOTALS
Municipal						
Canada	40		120	190	660	1010
	36		107	170	589	902
U.S.*	70	2940	310	2820	380	6520
**	62	2262	277	2515	339	5455
Total*	110	2940	430	3010	1040	7530
**	98	2622	384	2685	927	6716
Manufacturing						
Canada*	860		1360	1900	2760	6880
**	767		1213	1694	2462	6136
U.S.*	410	9650	1060	9110	530	20760
**	366	8608	945	8126	473	18518
Total*	1270	9650	2420	11010	3290	27640
**	1133	8608	2158	9820	2935	24652
Power Production						
Canada*	70		2870	1160	8370	12470
**	62		2560	1035	7466	11123
U.S.*	760	13600	2570	13180	6520	36360
**	678	12131	2292	11757	5816	32674
Total*	830	13600	5440	14340	14890	49100
**	740	12131	4852	12791	13282	43796
GRAND TOTALS						
	2210	26190	8290	28360	19220	84270
	1971	23361	7394	25296	17144	75166

Great Lakes Factsheet No. 3B
Water Consumed

	Superior	Michigan	Huron	Erie	Ontario	TOTALS
Municipal						
Canada	10		20	30	100	160
	9		18	27	89	143
U.S.*	10	190	170	280	70	720
**	9	169	152	257	62	649
Total*	20	190	190	210	170	780
**	18	169	170	189	152	698
Manufacturing						
Canada*	20		70	80	100	270
**	18		62	71	89	240
U.S.*	60	880	30	1500	40	2510
**	53	785	27	1338	36	2239
Total*	80	880	100	1580	140	2780
**	71	785	89	1409	125	2479
Power Production						
Canada*	0		20	10	60	90
**	0		18	9	54	81
U.S.*	10	240	50	190	120	610
**	9	214	45	169	108	545
Total*	10	240	70	200	180	700
**	9	214	62	178	174	673
GRAND TOTALS						
	110	1310	360	1990	490	4260
	98	1168	321	1776	451	3814

Cubic feet per second
Millions of cubic metres per year

Source: BULLETINS E-1866-70, Sea Grant College Program, Cooperative Extension Service, Michigan State University, E. Lansing, Michigan, 1985.

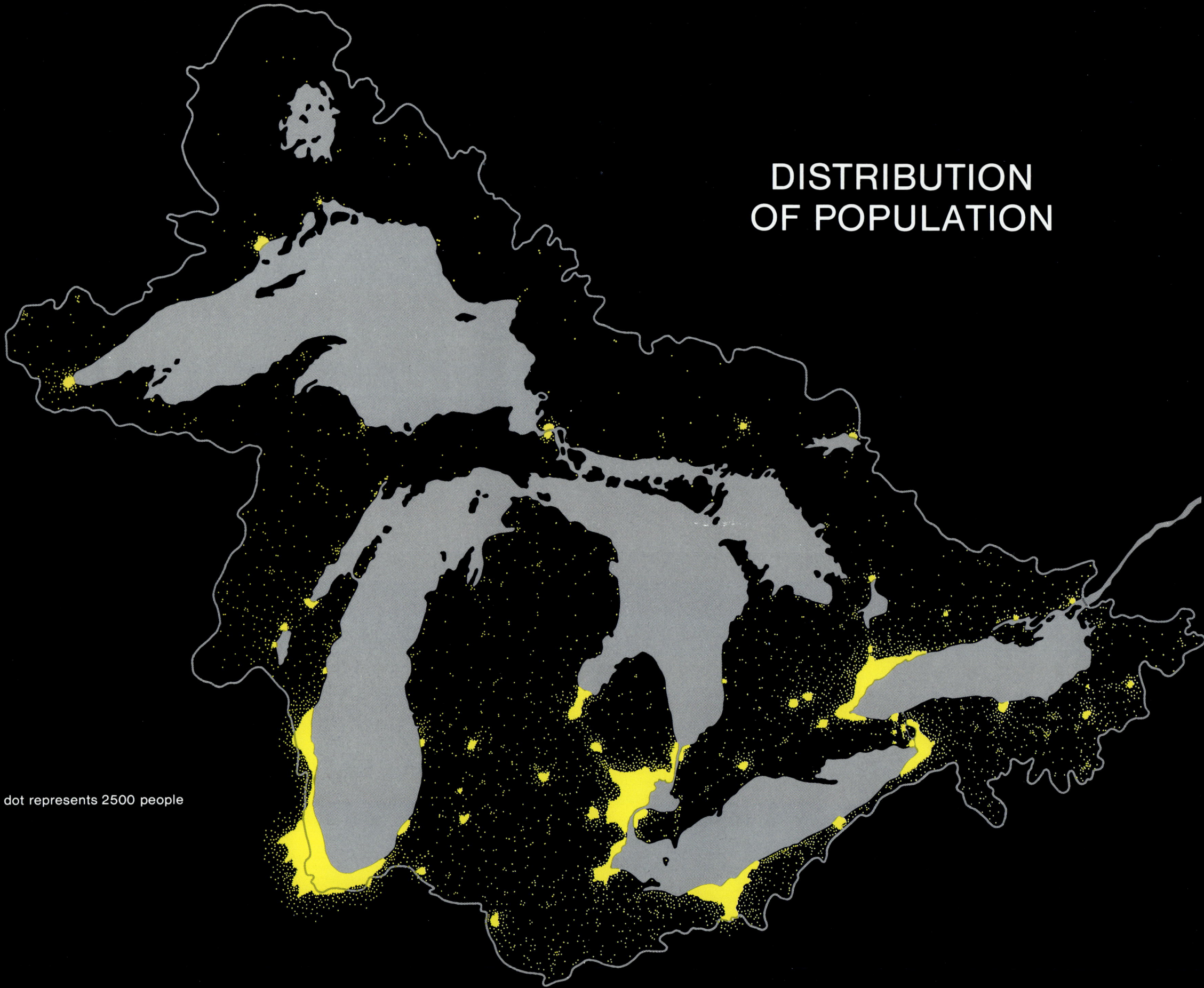

DISTRIBUTION
OF POPULATION

1 dot represents 2500 people

CHAPTER FOUR

THE GREAT LAKES TODAY — CONCERNS

Wilderness is the raw material out of which man has hammered the artifact called civilization …
No living man will see again the virgin pineries of the Lake states, or the flatwoods of the coastal plain, or the giant hardwoods …

- Aldo Leopold

While parts of the Great Lakes ecosystem have been changed to better suit the needs of humans, the unexpected consequences of many of the changes have only recently become apparent. Since 1960, the magnitude of these changes and the harsher implications of some human activities have slowly become better understood.

Deterioration in water quality began with modern settlement. At first the pollution was localized. Agricultural development, forestry and urbanization caused streams and shoreline marshes to silt up and harbor areas to become septic. Domestic and industrial waste discharges, occasional oil and chemical spills and the effects of mining left some parts of the waterways unfit for water supply and recreation. Waste-treatment solutions were adopted to treat biological pollutants which threatened the immediate health of populations. In some jurisdictions, regulations were passed to prevent capricious dumping in the waterways. Eventually, however, it took a major threat to the whole Great Lakes basin to awaken authorities to the fact that the entire Great Lakes ecosystem was being damaged.

PATHOGENS

Historically, the primary reason for water pollution control was prevention of waterborne disease. Municipalities began treating drinking water by adding chlorine, a disinfectant. This proved to be a simple solution to a very serious public health problem.

Humans can acquire bacterial, viral and parasitic diseases through direct body contact with contaminated water as well as by drinking the water. Preventing disease transmission of this kind usually means closing beaches during the summer when the water is warm and when bacteria from human feces reach higher concentrations. For instance, many of the public swimming beaches in the Toronto - Niagara area on Lake Ontario are closed for some or all of the summer because their bacterial count exceeds the safe level established by public health authorities. This is usually attributed to the common practice of combining storm and sanitary sewers in urban areas. Although this practice has been discontinued, existing combined sewers contribute to contamination problems during periods of high rainfall and urban runoff. At these times sewage treatment plants cannot handle the large volumes of combined storm and sanitary flow. The result is that untreated effluent, diluted by urban runoff, is discharged directly into waterways.

Modern, large-scale agriculture with its reliance on synthetic fertilizers and pesticides is one of the main nonpoint sources of pollution to the Great Lakes.

Remedial action can be very costly if the preferred solution is replacement of the dual-purpose systems in urban areas with separate storm and sanitary sewers. However, alternate techniques can be used which would greatly reduce the problem at lower costs. In the U.S., beach closures have become rare since sewage treatment was improved in the 1970s.

EUTROPHICATION and OXYGEN DEPLETION

Lakes can be characterized by their biological productivity, that is, the amount of living material supported within them, primarily in the form of algae. The least productive lakes are called oligotrophic; those with intermediate productivity are mesotrophic; and the most productive are eutrophic. The variables that determine productivity are temperature, light, depth and volume, and the amount of nutrients received from the environment.

Except in shallow bays and shoreline marshes, the Great Lakes were oligotrophic before European settlement and industrialization. Their size, depth and the climate kept them continuously cool and clear. The lakes received small amounts of fertilizers such as phosphorus and nitrogen from decomposing organic material in runoff from forested lands. Small amounts of nitrogen and phosphorus also came from the atmosphere.

These conditions have changed. Temperatures of some tributaries have been increased by thermal pollution and by removal of vegetative shade cover. But, more importantly, the amount of nutrients and organic material entering the lakes has increased with intensified urbanization and agriculture. Nutrient loading increased with the advent of phosphate detergents and inorganic fertilizers. Although controlled in most jurisdictions bordering the Great Lakes, phosphates in detergents continue to be a problem where they are not regulated.

Increased nutrients in the lakes stimulate the growth of green plants including algae. The amount of plant growth increases rapidly in the same way that applying lawn fertilizers (nitrogen, phosphorus and potassium) results in rapid, green growth. In the aquatic system the increased plant life eventually dies, settles to the bottom and decomposes. During decomposition, the organisms which break down the plants use up oxygen dissolved in the water near the bottom. With more growth there is more material to be decomposed, and more consumption of oxygen. Under normal conditions, when nutrient loadings are low, dissolved oxygen levels are kept high by the diffusion of oxygen into water, mixing by currents and wave action, and by the oxygen production of photosynthesizing plants.

Depletion of oxygen through decomposition of organic material is known as biochemical oxygen demand (BOD) which is generated from two different sources. In nearshore areas it is often caused by materials contained in the discharges from treatment plants. The other principal source is decaying algae. In deep-water areas such as the central basin of Lake Erie, algal BOD is the primary problem.

As the BOD load increases and as oxygen levels drop, certain species of fish can be killed and pollution-tolerant species that require less oxygen such as sludge worms and carp replace the original species. Changes in species of algae, bottom-dwelling organisms (or benthos), and fish are therefore good biological indicators of oxygen depletion. Turbidity in the water as well as an increase in chlorophyll also accompany accelerated algal growth and indicate increased eutrophication.

Lake Erie was the first of the Great Lakes to demonstrate a serious problem of eutrophication because it is the shallowest, warmest and naturally most productive. Lake Erie also experienced early and intense development of its lands for agricultural and urban uses. About one-third of the total Great Lakes basin population lives within its drainage area and surpasses all other lakes in the receipt of effluent from sewage treatment plants.

Oxygen depletion in the shallow central basin of Lake Erie was first reported in the late 1920s. Studies showed that the area of oxygen depletion grew larger with time, although the extent varied from year to year due, at least in part, to weather conditions. Eutrophication was believed to be the primary cause. Before controls could be developed, it was necessary to determine which nutrient(s) was (were) most important in causing eutrophication in previously mesotrophic or oligotrophic waters. By the late 1960s, the scientific consensus was that phosphorus was the key nutrient in the Great Lakes and that controlling the input of phosphorus could reduce eutrophication.

The central basin of Lake Erie is especially susceptible to depletion of oxygen in waters near the bottom because it stratifies in summer, forming a relatively thin layer of cool water, the hypolimnion, which is isolated from oxygen-rich surface waters. Oxygen is rapidly depleted from this thin layer as a result of decomposition of organic matter. When dissolved oxygen levels reach zero, the waters are considered to be anoxic. With anoxia many chemical processes change and previously oxidized pollutants may be altered to forms that are more readily available for uptake by the water. By contrast, the western basin of the lake is not generally susceptible to anoxia because the wind keeps the shallow basin well mixed, preventing complete stratification. The eastern basin is deeper and the thick hypolimnion contains enough oxygen to prevent anoxia.

In both Canada and the United States, the belief that Lake Erie was "dying" increased public alarm about water pollution everywhere. Even the casual observer could see that the lake was in trouble. Cladophora, a filamentous blue-green algae which thrives under eutrophic conditions, became the dominant nearshore algae covering beaches in green, slimy masses. Increased turbidity caused the lake to appear greenish-brown and murky.

In response to public concern, new pollution control laws were adopted in both countries to deal with water quality problems including phosphorus loadings to the lakes. In 1972, Canada and the United States signed the Great Lakes Water Quality Agreement to begin a binational Great Lakes cleanup that emphasized the reduction of phosphorus entering the lakes.

The concerted effort to reduce phosphorus loadings which began in 1972 represents an unprecedented international accomplishment. Loadings have been reduced by an estimated 80 to 90 percent through regulation and financial assistance, primarily for upgrading sewage treatment plants. Reductions in levels of phosphorus from industry and in domestic laundry detergents have also contributed. These reductions have resulted in dramatic improvements in nearshore water quality and some improvement in open lake conditions.

In 1983, the two countries approved a supplement to the Great Lakes Water Quality Agreement confirming the maximum phosphorus loads that the lakes could tolerate and agreed to prepare load reduction plans to achieve further reductions. Reduction in nonpoint sources is now the major focus of the plans.

The carcinogenic effects of toxic pollutants are believed to have caused this tumor (ossifying fibroma) on a sauger from the Great Lakes.

TOXIC CONTAMINANTS

Toxic contamination of the environment and the potential risk to human health have been the result of the increased commercial production and wide-spread use of synthetic organic chemicals and metals since the 1940s. The dangers of toxic substances in the natural environment were first illustrated through the study of the persistence, movement and effects of the pesticide DDT in the environment.

Toxic contaminants are the focus of concern in the 1978 Great Lakes Water Quality Agreement, the Great Lakes cleanup efforts of the International Joint Commission, and governments in both countries. Both governments have been urged to strengthen control of toxic substances by the Water Quality Board in a 1985 report and the Royal Society/U.S. National Academy of Sciences in a review of the 1978 Water Quality Agreement.

Toxic pollutants include man-made organic chemicals and heavy metals that can be acutely poisonous in relatively small amounts and injurious through chronic exposure in minute concentrations. Many trace contaminants that are present have the potential to increase the risk of cancer, birth defects and genetic mutations through long-term exposure. These chemicals may also be affecting aquatic organisms in the lakes.

The crossed bill of this Cormorant is believed to be an effect of toxic contamination of the food chain in isolated locations on the lakes.

Many toxic substances tend to bioaccumulate as they pass up the food chain in the aquatic ecosystem. While the concentrations in water of chemicals such as PCBs may be so low that the toxic substances are almost undetectable, biomagnification through the food chain can increase levels in predator fish such as large trout and salmon by a million times. Still further biomagnification occurs in birds and other animals that eat fish. Public health and environmental agencies in the Great Lakes states and the Province of Ontario warn against human consumption of certain fish. Some fish cannot be sold commercially because of high levels of PCBs, mercury or other substances.

Fish consumption provides a greater potential for exposure of humans to toxic substances from the Great Lakes than other activities such as drinking water or swimming. For example, a person who eats one meal of lake trout from Lake Michigan will be exposed to more PCBs in one meal than in a lifetime of drinking water from the lake. Epidemiological studies of Michigan residents have shown that people who regularly eat fish with high levels of PCBs have much higher concentrations in their bodies than others. The health risks of such exposure are uncertain but in one study, mothers who regularly ate fish with high PCB concentrations had higher levels of PCBs in their bodies and breast milk than mothers who did not regularly eat Great Lakes fish. Furthermore, the average birth weight of the infants exposed to more PCBs was smaller and their vital signs at birth were not as strong.

Sign on the Grand Calumet River, Indiana.

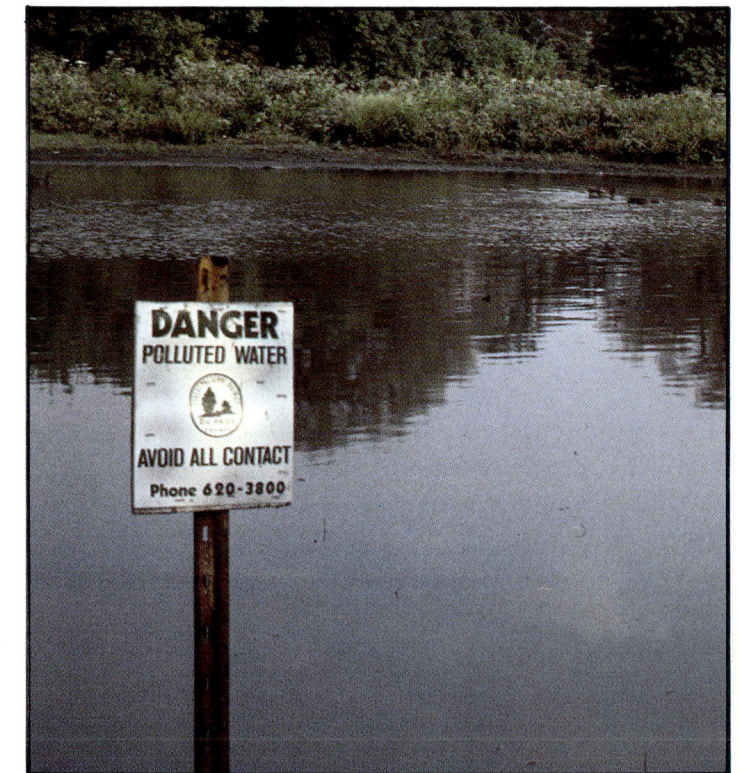

PATHWAYS OF POLLUTION

While efforts were underway to reduce point sources of pollution and to study nonpoint pollution sources, it was discovered that many pollutants are deposited from the atmosphere. Like the precursors of acid rain which can originate far from where the damage occurs, nutrients and toxic contaminants can be carried long distances from their sources to be deposited in the lakes in wet and dry forms. Atmospheric deposition of a pollutant in the Great Lakes basin was first recognized with phosphorus. Measurements of rain, snow and dust fall showed that about 20 percent of the phosphorus loading to Lake Michigan was from the atmosphere. Because this source could not be controlled, the need to reduce phosphorous in detergents, in sewage treatment, and from fertilizer runoff was reinforced. Atmospheric deposition of toxic chemicals was recognized by measurements of PCBs in precipitation after these chemicals were discovered in Great Lakes fish in 1971. Long-range transportation of substances was confirmed by the PCBs and toxaphene discovered in fish from a lake on Isle Royale, a remote island in Lake Superior isolated from any known direct sources of the pollutants.

Sediments which were contaminated before pollutant discharges were regulated are another source of pollution. Such in-place pollutants are a problem in most urban-industrial areas. Release of pollutants from sediments is believed to be occurring in connecting channels such as the Niagara, St. Clair and St. Marys rivers, in harbors such as Hamilton, Toronto and the Grand Calumet, and in tributaries such as the Buffalo, Ashtabula and Black rivers. Even where it is possible to remove highly contaminated sediments from harbors, removal can cause problems when sediments are placed in landfills which may later leak and contaminate wetlands and groundwater. Dredging for navigation can also present problems of disposal of dredge spoils. Disposal of highly polluted sediments in the open lakes has been prohibited since the 1960s.

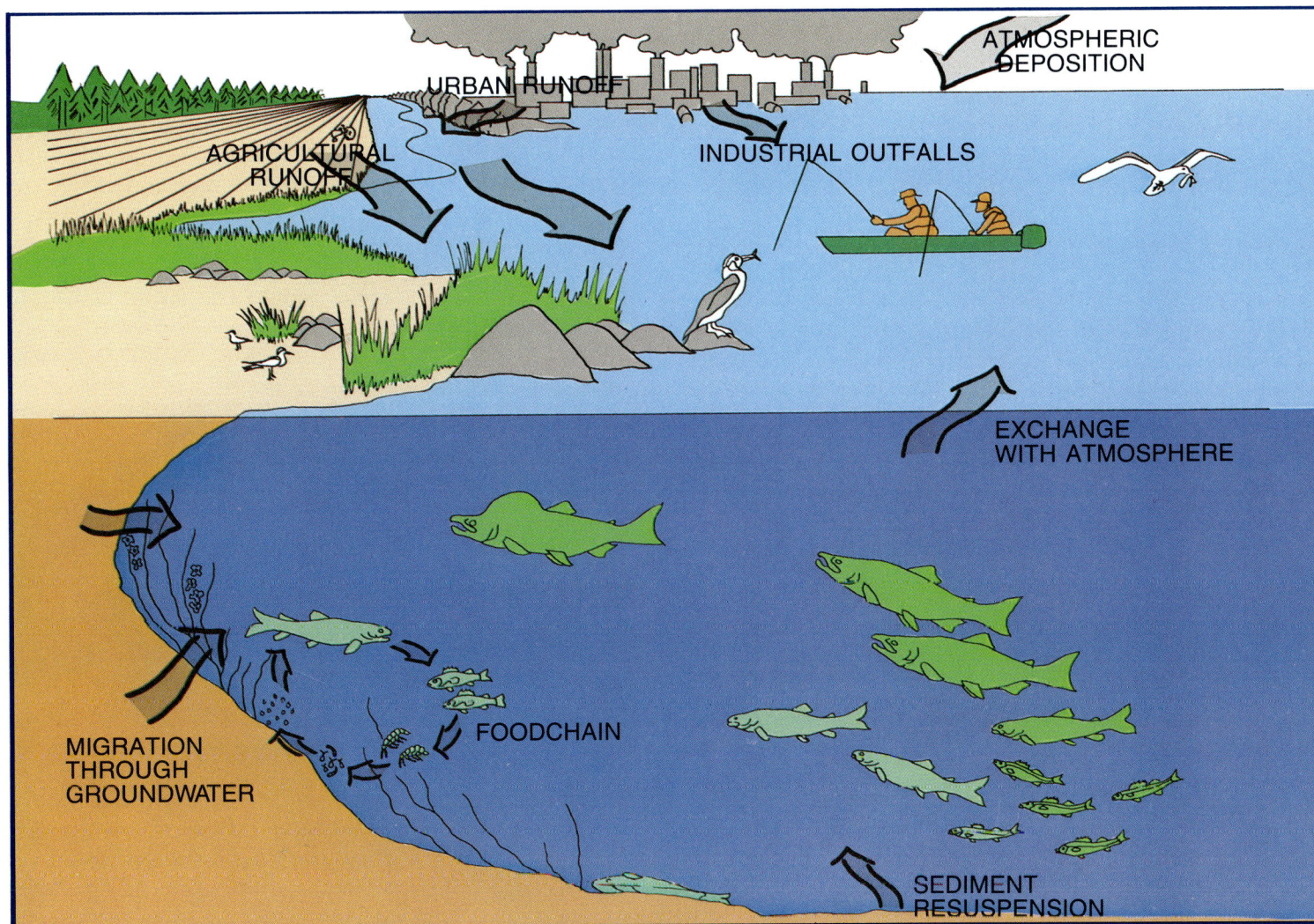

Dredging   Shipping   Storms

Biotic Disturbances

SEDIMENT RESUSPENSION. Polluted sediments that have settled out of the water can be stirred up and resuspended in water by dredging, by the passage of ships in navigation channels, and by wind and wave action. Sediments can also be disturbed by fish and other organisms that feed on the bottom.

ATMOSPHERIC DEPOSITION

URBAN RUNOFF

AGRICULTURAL RUNOFF

INDUSTRIAL OUTFALLS

EXCHANGE WITH ATMOSPHERE

MIGRATION THROUGH GROUNDWATER

FOODCHAIN

SEDIMENT RESUSPENSION

SOURCES AND PATHWAYS OF POLLUTION.

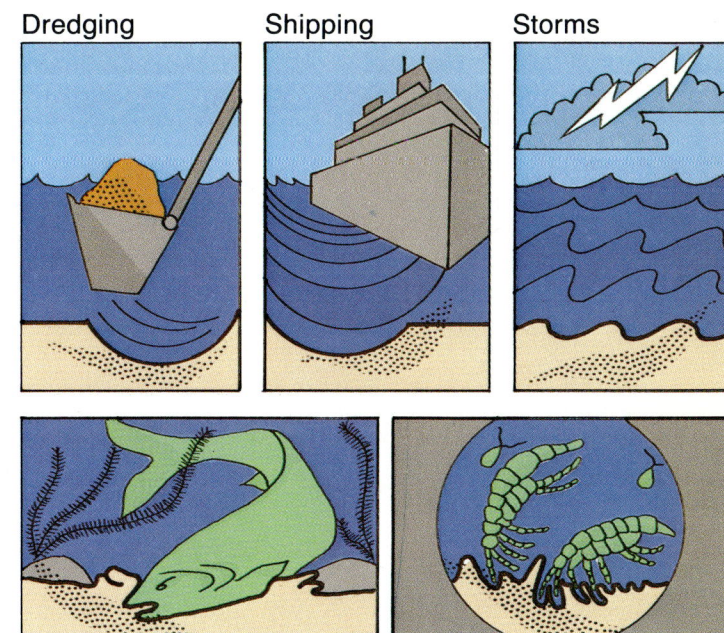

Groundwater movement is another pathway for pollutants. As water slowly passes through the ground it picks up materials that are buried. Near-surface disposal sites along the Niagara River have been found to be leaking a wide variety of toxic substances into the river which then flows into Lake Ontario. Fissures in the bedrock allow substances to migrate with ground water to the walls of the Niagara Gorge where they then flow to the river. Results of a study conducted in late 1985 suggest that industrial wastes may be contaminating ground water around a railway tunnel on the Canadian side of the St. Clair River. A possible source could be wastes from the former disposal zone in the bedrock beneath the Sarnia area.

Surface runoff is the pathway for a wide variety of substances to enter the lakes. Nutrients, pesticides and soils are released by agricultural activities. In urban areas, street runoff includes automobile-related substances such as salt, sand, asbestos, lead, oils and greases. Surface runoff also includes a wide number of materials deposited with precipitation which may include particulates, bacteria, nutrients and toxic substances.

BIOACCUMULATION and BIOMAGNIFICATION

The nutrients necessary for plant growth (eg., nitrogen and phosphorus) are found at very low concentrations in most natural waters. In order to obtain sufficient quantities for growth, phytoplankton must collect these chemical elements from a relatively large volume of water.

In the process of collecting nutrients, they also collect certain man-made chemicals, such as some persistent pesticides. These may be present in the water at concentrations so low that they cannot be measured even by very sensitive instruments. The chemicals, however, biologically accumulate (bioaccumulate) in the organism and become concentrated at levels which are much higher in the living cells than in the open water. This is especially true for persistent chemicals - substances that do not break down readily in the environment - like DDT and PCBs that are stored in fatty tissues.

The small fish and zooplankton eat vast quantities of phytoplankton. In doing so any toxic chemicals accumulated by the phytoplankton are further concentrated in the bodies of the animals that eat them. This is repeated at each step in the food chain. This process of increasing concentration through the foodchain is known as biomagnification.

The top predators at the end of a long food chain, such as lake trout, large salmon and fish-eating gulls, may accumulate concentrations of a toxic chemical high enough to cause serious deformities or death even though the concentration of the chemical in the open water is extremely low. The concentration of some chemicals in the fatty tissues of top predators can be a million times higher than the concentration in the open water.

The eggs of aquatic birds often have some of the highest concentrations of toxic chemicals, because they are at the end of a long aquatic food chain, and because egg yolk is rich in fatty material. Thus, the first apparent effects of a toxic chemical in a lake appear as dead or malformed chicks. Scientists monitor colonies of gulls and other water birds because these effects can serve as early warning signs of a growing toxic chemical problem. They also collect gull eggs for chemical analysis because toxic chemicals will be detectable in them long before they reach measurable levels in the open water. Research of this kind is important because humans are consumers in the Great Lakes foodchain.

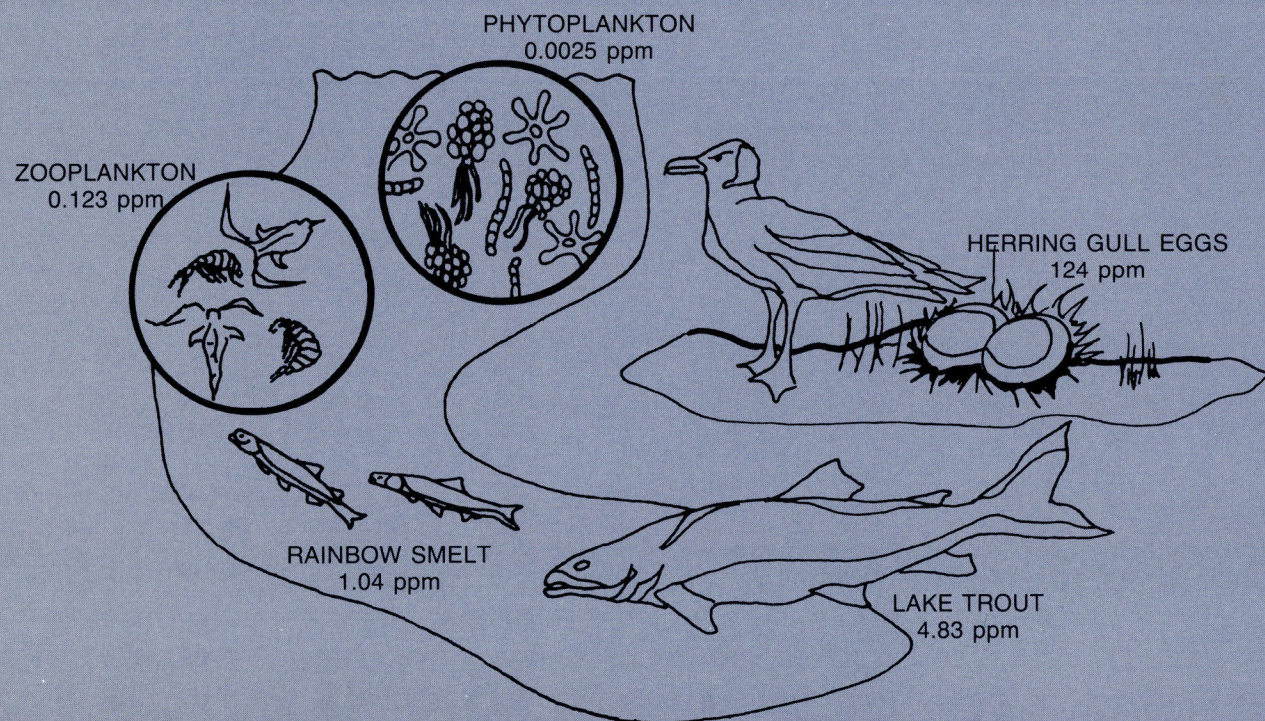

PHYTOPLANKTON
0.0025 ppm

ZOOPLANKTON
0.123 ppm

HERRING GULL EGGS
124 ppm

RAINBOW SMELT
1.04 ppm

LAKE TROUT
4.83 ppm

PERSISTENT ORGANIC CHEMICALS such as PCBs, bioaccumulate. This diagram shows the degree of concentration in each level of the Great Lakes aquatic foodchain for PCBs (in parts per million, ppm). The highest levels are reached in the eggs of fish-eating birds such as herring gulls.

Some of the chemicals found in the lakes are believed to be cancer-causing agents, carcinogens. The identification of a carcinogen through public health studies is often difficult because many years may elapse between exposure to the chemical cause and development of a tumor. Establishment of cause and effect relationships is also complicated by interactions between substances which can either interfere with (by antagonism) or enhance (by synergism) the action of a given carcinogen.

As the understanding of how toxic substances cycle in the ecosystem has grown, steps have been taken to control or prevent their introduction into the environment. The most common approach has been to ban the production and use of certain individual chemicals and metals and to prevent the direct discharge of others into waterways. The production and use of DDT were banned after it was shown how the pesticide thins the shells of bird eggs causing reproductive failures. The levels of DDT in the environment began to decline immediately following regulation. In the case of PCBs, production has been banned but their use is still being phased out.

SOURCES OF POLLUTANTS

In general there are two ways to characterize the sources of pollutants. Point sources are direct discharges from identifiable and concentrated inputs such as municipal sewer outfalls or industrial discharges. Nonpoint sources are diffuse inputs such as from land runoff or the atmosphere. Examples of nonpoint source pollutants are agricultural runoff, automobile emissions and pollutants released from disposal sites.

Point source pollutants are generally less difficult to control because they tend to be concentrated. For instance, waste water from industries, municipalities, and thermal generating stations can be treated by containment and removal of the harmful substances. However, the disposal of resultant waste materials can become a non-point source problem if they are incinerated, stored on land or buried in waste disposal sites. The dispersed pathways from nonpoint sources are poorly understood and controls are technically and institutionally difficult, and often expensive.

INTERNATIONAL JOINT COMMISSION AREAS OF CONCERN

Overall, water quality in the lakes is improving due to the progress which has been made in controlling direct discharges of wastes from municipalities and industries under environmental laws adopted since the 1960s. Even so, some areas still suffer serious impairment of beneficial uses (drinking, fishing, swimming, etc.) and fail to meet environmental standards and objectives.

FISH ADVISORIES

The state and provincial governments surrounding the Great Lakes have issued advisories for people consuming fish caught in the lakes. These advisories suggest that consumption of certain species and sizes of fish should be avoided or reduced due to toxic chemicals present in the fish. These chemicals can cause a number of human health problems ranging from cancer to birth defects and neurological disorders.

As a result of uncertainty in the scientific community about the toxicity to humans of these chemicals, the jurisdictions surrounding the lakes vary in the advice they provide. However, in all cases, following the advisories will reduce (but not necessarily eliminate) the exposure and, therefore, the risk of suffering adverse effects. High-risk groups such as pregnant women, nursing mothers and pre-teen children are advised to pay close attention to the advisories.

For more information, consumers should contact their public health and environmental agencies before eating fish from the Great Lakes or their tributaries.

Serious problems remain throughout the basin in locations identified by the International Joint Commission as 'areas of concern'. Areas of concern are those geographic areas where beneficial use of water or biota is adversely affected or where environmental criteria are exceeded to the extent that use impairment is likely to exist. The purpose of establishing areas of concern is to encourage jurisdictions to rehabilitate these acute, localized problem areas and to restore their beneficial uses. The areas are classified according to their stage in the remedial process. In these areas, existing routine programs are not expected to be sufficient to restore water quality to acceptable levels. Jurisdictions are preparing remedial action plans to guide specific rehabilitation activities in all 42 areas.

Most IJC areas of concern are near the mouths of tributaries where cities and industries are located. Several of the areas are along the connecting channels of the St. Clair and Niagara Rivers. Pollutants are concentrated in these areas because of long term, direct discharge of wastes from local sources, nonpoint source leaching of contaminants and accumulation of pollutants from upstream. Nearly all the areas of concern have contaminated sediments.

Over the last decade, the nature of the problems associated with some areas has changed. For instance, as progress was made in restoring dissolved oxygen and reducing some toxics such as lead and mercury, it became apparent that the problem of dissolved oxygen had been obscuring other problems of toxic contamination. In these areas, continued remedial action and research is necessary.

Understanding all the sources, fates and effects of toxic contaminants in the Great Lakes ecosystem is still at a relatively early stage. Governmental programs to address toxic substances are progressing and attempting to bring current sources under control to levels that protect human health. However, it is not clear that such levels are fully effective in the rehabilitation of the Great Lakes with their long food chains and high degree of bioaccumulation. Also, toxic chemicals released during earlier less regulated times remain within the system and continue to create problems.

In some cases, levels have declined for substances whose production has been banned or whose use has been restricted. These include DDT, PCBs, mirex and mercury. However, with hundreds of other chemicals remaining in the ecosystem and many new ones being found annually, it can be expected that new problems will continue to develop.

OTHER BASIN CONCERNS

Acid precipitation created by continued use of fossil fuels in the transportation sector and in the production of electrical power, as well as from smelter emissions, may seriously affect the quality of aquatic ecosystems. Small lakes and tributaries which feed the Great Lakes are most susceptible. Because of the underlying sedimentary limestone in most of the basin, the Great Lakes have a natural capacity to buffer the effects of acid rain. However, concern remains for the lakes and tributaries originating in the northern forest on the Canadian Shield. In Ontario, Minnesota and Michigan acidification is already evident in many small lakes.

Wetlands are another concern. Many natural wetlands have been filled in or drained throughout the southern part of the region for agriculture, urban uses, shoreline development, recreation and resource extraction (peat mining). It is estimated, for example, that between 70 and 80 percent of the original wetlands of Southern Ontario have been lost since European settlement. Governments continue to encourage this practice through drainage subsidies to farmers. The loss of these lands poses special problems for hydrological processes and water quality because of the natural storage and cleansing functions of wetlands. Moreover, the loss makes difficult the preservation and protection of certain wildlife species such as fish and waterfowl.

The shoreline of the Great Lakes is under continual stress. In the lower lakes region little remains undeveloped. Most lakefront properties are in private ownership and thus under limited control by public authorities wishing to protect them. Erosion losses are high because of intensive development and loss of vegetative cover and other natural protection. Damages due to flooding are also of concern, particularly during

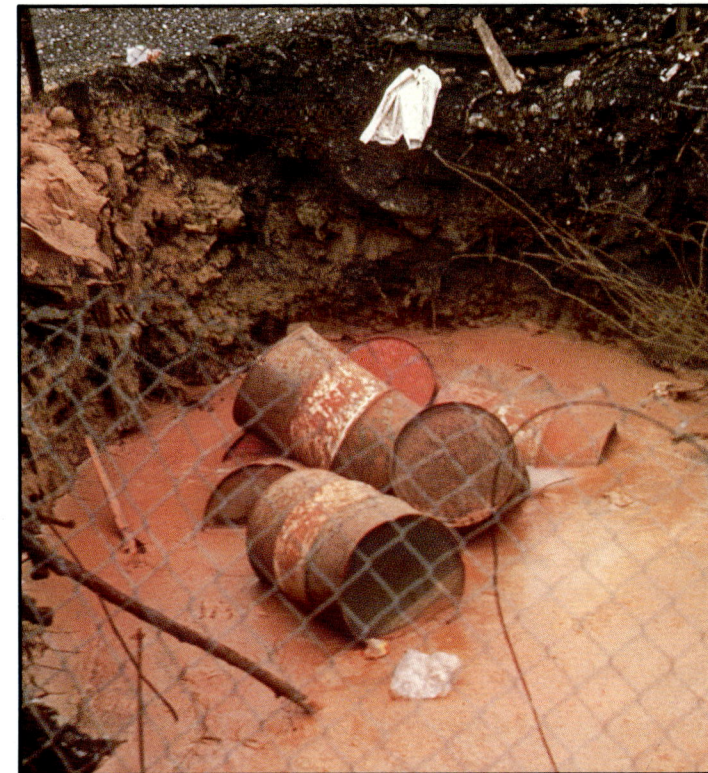

Improper storage of toxic contaminants leads to contamination of the groundwater supply which can have far-reaching effects.

periods of high lake levels. Flooding and erosion damages to private property lead to public pressure on governments to further regulate lake levels through diversion manipulation and control structures on outlet channels (see Chapter Three.) The demand for public access to the lakes for recreation has grown steadily in recent years and can be projected to continue. Currently, the greatest growth is in the development of marinas for recreational boating.

Some consideration has been given to the sale of water as a commodity to fast-growing water-poor areas such as the American Midwest and Southwest. These range from proposals for minor diversions out of the basin to mega-projects which would see large-scale alterations to the natural flows from as far away as James Bay, through the Great Lakes basin, to the American sunbelt states. Opposition to such suggestions comes from environmentalists and others who fear the enormous consequences of such large-scale manipulation of the natural watersheds.

It would be a tragic irony if, because of our failure to deal with the pollution of the lakes and the effects of our development of the basin, we look out over the vast expanse of the lakes and realize that we have permanently damaged a sustaining natural resource.

POLLUTION SOURCES AND TROPHIC STATUS

TROPHIC STATUS

- Oligotrophic
- Oligotrophic/Mesotrophic
- Mesotrophic
- Mesotrophic/Eutrophic
- Eutrophic

Data available for Great Lakes coastal areas only. Coastal bands not drawn to scale.

AREAS OF CONCERN

◆

Areas of concern are areas such as harbours, river mouths and connecting channels exhibiting serious environmental degradation, according to the Great Lakes Water Quality Board and the International Joint Commission.

POLLUTION SOURCES

- ● **Main map and inset map:** Waste discharges in excess of operating permits, according to Pollution Probe.

- ● **Inset map only:** Waste discharges providing a significant loading into the water, according to the Niagara River Toxics Committee. Some of these discharges also fall into the previous category.

- ● **Main map and inset map:** Hazardous waste sites having the greatest potential impact on human health and the environment, according to the Ontario Ministry of the Environment and the United States Environmental Protection Agency "Superfund" National Priorities List.

- ● **Inset map only:** Hazardous waste sites having significant potential for contaminant migration, according to the Niagara River Toxics Committee. Some of these sites also fall into the previous category.

NOTE:
The various government agencies responsible for the source data use different definitions and significance levels; thus not all the sites shown are equally threatening to human health and the environment.

NIAGARA RIVER AREA

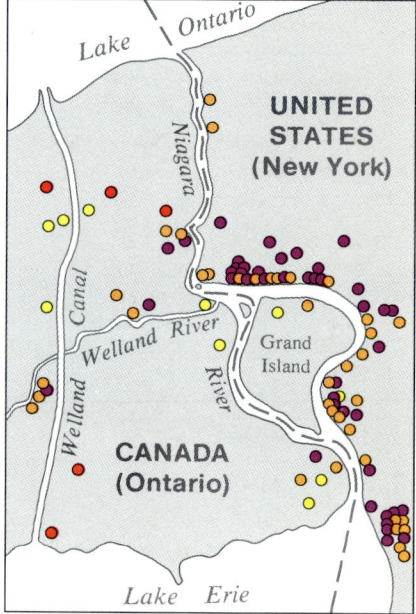

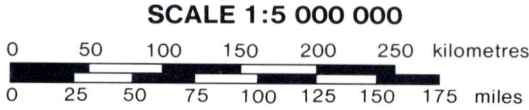

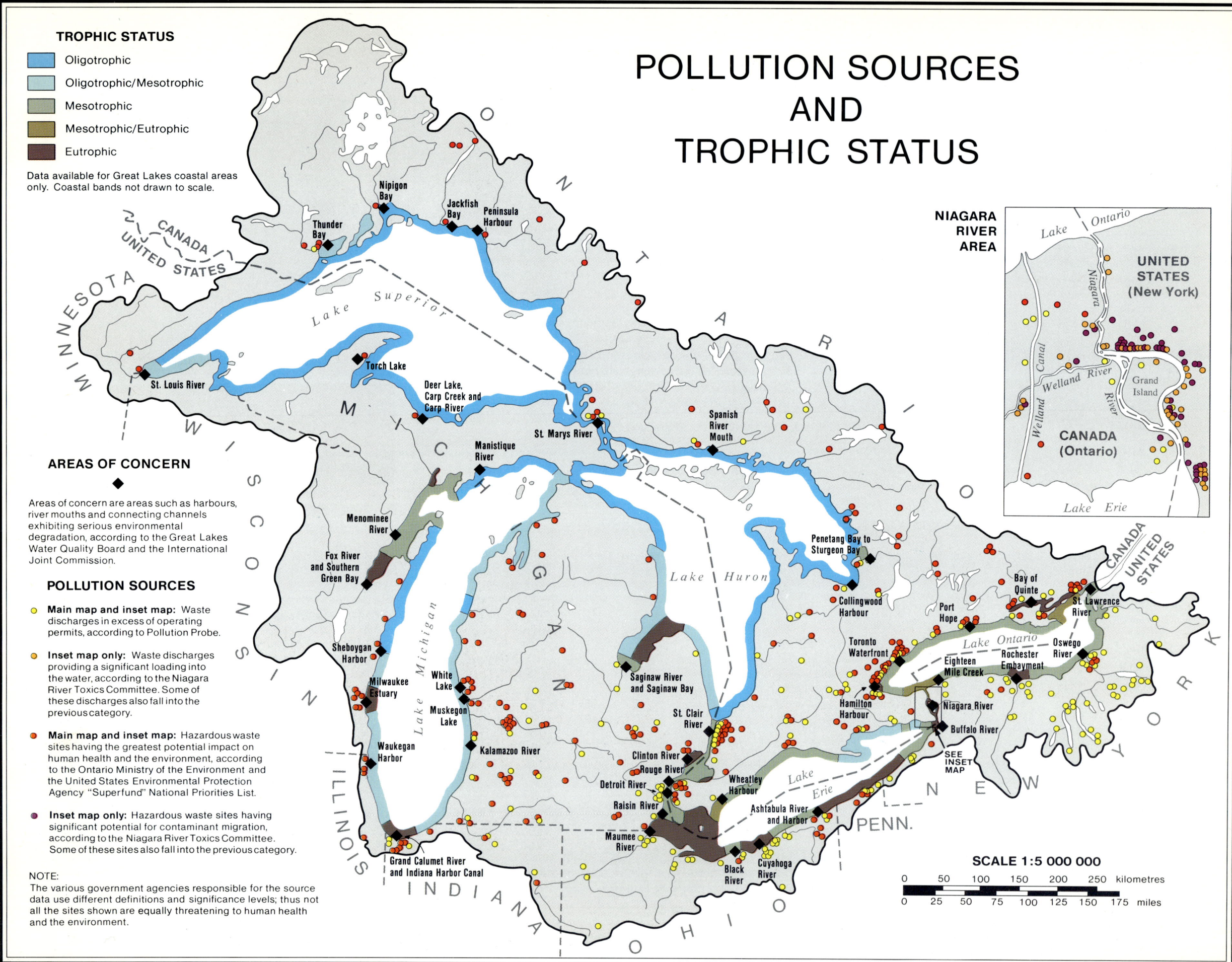

SCALE 1:5 000 000

| 0 | 50 | 100 | 150 | 200 | 250 kilometres |

| 0 | 25 | 50 | 75 | 100 | 125 | 150 | 175 miles |

GREAT LAKES FACT SHEET NO. 4   INTERNATIONAL JOINT COMMISSION AREAS OF CONCERN: POLLUTION PROBLEMS AND SOURCES

LAKE BASIN/ AREA OF CONCERN	JURISDICTION	TYPES OF PROBLEMS						SOURCES OF POLLUTION			
		Conventional Pollutants	Heavy Metals and Toxic Organics	Contaminated Sediments	Eutrophication	Biological Impacts and Fish Advisories	Beach Closings	Nonpoint Sources	Municipal Industrial Point Sources	Waste Disposal Sites	In-Place Pollutants
LAKE SUPERIOR											
Peninsula Harbour	Ontario										
Jackfish Bay	Ontario										
Nipigon Bay	Ontario										
Thunder Bay	Ontario										
St. Louis River	Minnesota										
Torch Lake	Michigan										
Deer Lake-Carp Creek-Carp River	Michigan										
LAKE MICHIGAN											
Manistique River	Michigan										
Menominee River	Michigan/Wisconsin										
Fox River/Southern Green Bay	Wisconsin										
Sheboygan	Wisconsin										
Milwaukee Estuary	Wisconsin										
Waukegan Harbor	Illinois										
Grand Calumet River/ Indiana Harbor Canal	Indiana										
Kalamazoo River	Michigan										
Muskegon Lake	Michigan										
White Lake	Michigan										
LAKE HURON											
Saginaw River/ Saginaw Bay	Michigan										
Collingwood Harbour	Ontario										
Penetang Bay to Sturgeon Bay	Ontario										
Spanish River Mouth	Ontario										
LAKE ERIE											
Clinton River	Michigan										
Rouge River	Michigan										
Raisin River	Ohio										
Maumee River	Ohio										
Black River	Ohio										
Cuyahoga River	Ohio										
Ashtabula River	Ohio										
Wheatley Harbour	Ontario										
LAKE ONTARIO											
Buffalo River	New York										
Eighteen Mile Creek	New York										
Rochester Embayment	New York										
Oswego River	New York										
Bay of Quinte	Ontario										
Port Hope	Ontario										
Toronto Waterfront	Ontario										
Hamilton Harbour	Ontario										
CONNECTING CHANNELS											
St. Marys River	Ontario/Michigan										
St. Clair River	Ontario/Michigan										
Detroit River	Ontario/Michigan										
Niagara River	Ontario/New York										
St. Lawrence River	Ontario/New York										

SOURCE: Adapted from IJC. 1985 REPORT ON GREAT LAKES WATER QUALITY. Report of the Water Quality Board. Kingston, Ont: 1985.

INTERNATIONAL JOINT COMMISSION AREAS OF CONCERN. The IJC has identified 42 areas where the use of water has been impaired by continuous pollution or where the objectives of the Great Lakes Water Quality Agreement and local standards are not being achieved. Studies and remedial action plans are being undertaken for many of the areas.

ECOREGIONS, WETLANDS AND DRAINAGE BASINS

MAJOR WETLANDS

There are numerous wetlands in northern Ontario and elsewhere that are too small to show individually at this scale.

NOTE:
Ecoregions are areas that exhibit broad ecological unity, based on such characteristics as climate, landforms, soils, vegetation, hydrology and wildlife.

CANADIAN ECOREGIONS

1	Lake St. Joseph Plains
2	Nipigon Plains
3	Thunder Bay Plains
4	Superior Highlands
5	Matagami
6	Chapleau Plains
7	Nipissing
8	Hurontario
9	Erie
10	Saint Laurent

DRAINAGE BASINS

— Great Lakes Basin
— Lake Basins
– – Sub Basins

UNITED STATES ECOREGIONS

11	Northeastern Highlands
12	Erie/Ontario Lake Plain
13	Northern Appalachian Plateau and Uplands
14	Eastern Corn Belt Plains
15	Huron/Erie Lake Plain
16	Southern Michigan/Northern Indiana Clay Plains
17	Central Corn Belt Plains
18	Southeastern Wisconsin Till Plain
19	North Central Hardwood Forests
20	Northern Lakes and Forests

SCALE 1:5 000 000

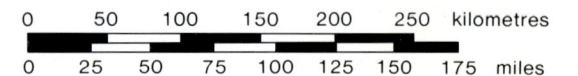

0 50 100 150 200 250 kilometres

0 25 50 75 100 125 150 175 miles

Map labels include: Ogoki River, Lake Nipigon, Long Lake, Dog River, Nipigon River, Pic River, White River, Magpie R., Isle Royale, LAKE SUPERIOR, Keweenaw Peninsula, St. Louis R., Escanaba River, Menominee River, Montreal River, Mississagi R., Spanish R., Wanapitei River, French R., Lake Nipissing, Magnetawan R., Muskoka R., St. Marys River, Straits of Mackinac, North Channel, Manitoulin Island, Georgian Bay, LAKE HURON, Lake Simcoe, Trent River, St. Lawrence River, Door Peninsula, Green Bay, Wolf R., Fox River, Lake Winnebago, LAKE MICHIGAN, Manistee River, Au Sable River, Saginaw Bay, Saginaw River, Muskegon River, Grand River, Saugeen R., Niagara River, Black River, LAKE ONTARIO, Oswego R., Genesee River, Grand River, St. Clair River, Thames, Lake St. Clair, Detroit River, LAKE ERIE, St. Joseph River, Maumee River, Sandusky River

CHAPTER FIVE

JOINT MANAGEMENT OF THE GREAT LAKES

The concept of an ecosystem approach to management of the Great Lakes has developed out of the joint experience of Canada and the United States. An evolution in understanding of how environmental damage has resulted from human use of natural resources in the basin has arisen out of the research, monitoring and commitment to Great Lakes protection by the governments and citizens of both countries.

Originally, water pollution was treated as a separate problem. As experience demonstrated connections between use of land, air and water resources, appreciation grew for the need to consider relationships within the ecosystem. Concern about protection and use of waters that are shared by the United States and Canada led to creation of institutions that foster joint management.

The first changes that became apparent due to intensive settlement and development were considered local and specific. Initially, solutions to problems such as bacterial contamination near cities, sedimentation of tributary mouths and industrial pollution were handled locally. Usually the solutions involved dilution or displacement of polluted discharges to other locations. Eventually pollution that had been local began to affect whole lakes and then became basin-wide concerns.

THE BOUNDARY WATERS TREATY OF 1909

In 1905 the International Waterways Commission was created to advise the governments of both countries about levels and flows in the Great Lakes, especially in relation to the generation of electricity by hydropower. Its limited advisory powers proved inadequate for problems related to pollution and environmental damage. One of its first recommendations was for a stronger institution with the authority for study of broader boundary water issues and the power to make binding decisions.

The Boundary Waters Treaty was signed in 1909 and provided for the creation of the International Joint Commission (IJC). The IJC has the authority to resolve disputes over the use of water resources that cross the international boundary. Most of its efforts for the Great Lakes have been devoted to carrying out studies requested by the governments and advising the governments about problems.

In 1912, water pollution was one of the first problems referred to the IJC for study. In 1919, after several years of study, the IJC concluded that serious water quality problems required a new treaty to control pollution. However, no agreement was reached.

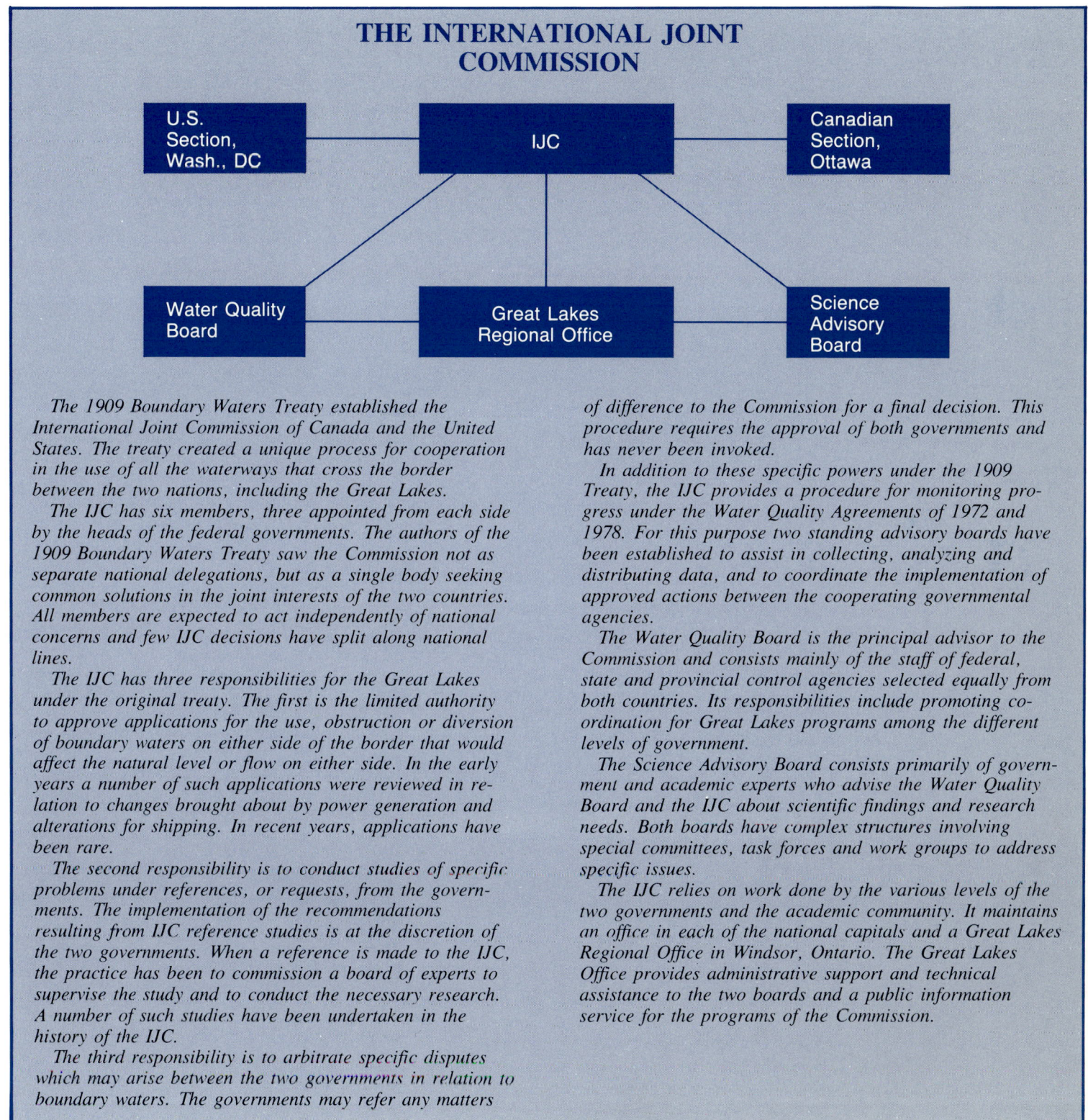

THE INTERNATIONAL JOINT COMMISSION

```
                              ┌─────────┐
┌──────────────┐              │         │              ┌──────────────┐
│ U.S.         │              │   IJC   │              │ Canadian     │
│ Section,     │──────────────│         │──────────────│ Section,     │
│ Wash., DC    │              │         │              │ Ottawa       │
└──────────────┘              └─────────┘              └──────────────┘

┌──────────────┐         ┌──────────────────┐          ┌──────────────┐
│ Water Quality│         │ Great Lakes      │          │ Science      │
│ Board        │         │ Regional Office  │          │ Advisory     │
│              │         │                  │          │ Board        │
└──────────────┘         └──────────────────┘          └──────────────┘
```

The 1909 Boundary Waters Treaty established the International Joint Commission of Canada and the United States. The treaty created a unique process for cooperation in the use of all the waterways that cross the border between the two nations, including the Great Lakes.

The IJC has six members, three appointed from each side by the heads of the federal governments. The authors of the 1909 Boundary Waters Treaty saw the Commission not as separate national delegations, but as a single body seeking common solutions in the joint interests of the two countries. All members are expected to act independently of national concerns and few IJC decisions have split along national lines.

The IJC has three responsibilities for the Great Lakes under the original treaty. The first is the limited authority to approve applications for the use, obstruction or diversion of boundary waters on either side of the border that would affect the natural level or flow on either side. In the early years a number of such applications were reviewed in relation to changes brought about by power generation and alterations for shipping. In recent years, applications have been rare.

The second responsibility is to conduct studies of specific problems under references, or requests, from the governments. The implementation of the recommendations resulting from IJC reference studies is at the discretion of the two governments. When a reference is made to the IJC, the practice has been to commission a board of experts to supervise the study and to conduct the necessary research. A number of such studies have been undertaken in the history of the IJC.

The third responsibility is to arbitrate specific disputes which may arise between the two governments in relation to boundary waters. The governments may refer any matters

of difference to the Commission for a final decision. This procedure requires the approval of both governments and has never been invoked.

In addition to these specific powers under the 1909 Treaty, the IJC provides a procedure for monitoring progress under the Water Quality Agreements of 1972 and 1978. For this purpose two standing advisory boards have been established to assist in collecting, analyzing and distributing data, and to coordinate the implementation of approved actions between the cooperating governmental agencies.

The Water Quality Board is the principal advisor to the Commission and consists mainly of the staff of federal, state and provincial control agencies selected equally from both countries. Its responsibilities include promoting coordination for Great Lakes programs among the different levels of government.

The Science Advisory Board consists primarily of government and academic experts who advise the Water Quality Board and the IJC about scientific findings and research needs. Both boards have complex structures involving special committees, task forces and work groups to address specific issues.

The IJC relies on work done by the various levels of the two governments and the academic community. It maintains an office in each of the national capitals and a Great Lakes Regional Office in Windsor, Ontario. The Great Lakes Office provides administrative support and technical assistance to the two boards and a public information service for the programs of the Commission.

NATIONAL INSTITUTIONAL ARRANGEMENTS FOR GREAT LAKES MANAGEMENT

The Great Lakes Water Quality Agreement recognizes that control procedures, research, and monitoring would continue to be conducted by the two countries within their respective legislative and administrative structures. Because of their obligations under the Agreement, both governments have established special programs for the Great Lakes.

In Canada, the British North America Act assigns the authority for navigable waters and international waters to the federal government, while pollution control and the management of natural resources are primarily provincial. Consequently, the initiative to establish water quality objectives under the Great Lakes Water Quality Agreement has been federal/provincial, while the implementation has been primarily a provincial responsibility.

The federal Canada Water Act provides for federal/provincial agreements setting out responsibilities for both levels of government. The Canada/Ontario Agreement provides for joint funding of activities required by the Great Lakes Water Quality Agreement and enables the federal government to play a greater role in pollution control.

The lead agency at the federal level is Environment Canada. It maintains research facilities at the Canada Centre for Inland Waters (CCIW) in Burlington, Ontario. CCIW houses laboratories and support services for Environment Canada's research effort. The department of Fisheries and Oceans is a major contributor of scientific and research support to Canada's Great Lakes program. Other federal departments directly involved include the Department of Health and Welfare, Agriculture Canada, Transport Canada, and the Department of Public Works.

The major responsibility for water quality at the provincial level rests with the Ontario Ministry of Environment (MOE). The MOE is responsible for establishing individual control orders for each industrial discharger. It also provides, along with the federal government, funding for municipal sewage treatment.

In the U.S., many federal environmental laws affect the lakes, including the Clean Water Act, the Resource Conservation and Recovery Act, the Toxic Substances Control Act, the Comprehensive Environmental Response and Recovery Act (Superfund) and the National Environmental Policy Act. These statutes provide federal regulatory authority, but it is federal policy to delegate regulatory authority to the state governments wherever possible. The states have their own laws and operate using both state and federal funding.

Two considerations determine the level of control required by U.S. laws. The first requires all municipal and industrial dischargers to meet minimum national standards for pollution control. Secondly, if further limits are necessary to meet ambient environmental standards, tighter limits can be imposed.

For meeting U.S. obligations under the Great Lakes Agreement, the U.S. Environmental Protection Agency (EPA) has the lead responsibility. Numerous other agencies also have important roles, particularly the U.S. Fish and Wildlife Service and the U.S. Coast Guard.

The federal government supports Great Lakes Research in several agencies. The Great Lakes National Program Office in the EPA regional office at Chicago provides funding for applied research and coordinates its activities with EPA research laboratories in Grosse Ile, Michigan, Duluth, Minnesota and elsewhere.

The National Oceanic and Atmospheric Administration (NOAA) has a Great Lakes Environmental Research Laboratory and the U.S. Fish and Wildlife Service maintains laboratories at the National Fisheries Center in Ann Arbor, Michigan. The Army Corps of Engineers carries out research on water quality as well as water quantity. A network of Sea Grant College programs is supported by state and federal funding at universities in seven of the Great Lakes states.

binational Great Lakes Fisheries Commission was established to find a means of control for the lamprey. By the late 1970s the lamprey population had been reduced by 90 percent with use of selective chemicals to kill the larvae in streams. Since then, the Fisheries Commission has expanded its activities to include work to rehabilitate the fisheries of the lakes and to coordinate government efforts to stock and restore fish populations.

Public and scientific concern about pollution of the lakes grew as accelerated eutrophication became more obvious through the 1950s. In 1964 the IJC began a new reference study on pollution in the lower Great Lakes. The report on this study in 1970 placed the principal blame for eutrophication on excessive phosphorus.

Fish kills of the type seen here prompted citizens to demand that remedial action be taken to improve water quality on the Great Lakes.

The study proposed basin-wide efforts to reduce phosphorus loadings from all sources. It was recognized that reduction of phosphorus depended on control of local sources. Uniform effluent limits were urged for all industries and municipal sewage treatment systems in the basin. Research suggested that land runoff could also be an important source of nutrients and other pollutants into the lakes. The result of the reference study was the signing of the first Great Lakes Water Quality Agreement in 1972.

Additional studies in the 1940s led to new concerns by the IJC. The commission recommended that water quality objectives be established for the Great Lakes and that technical advisory boards be created to provide continuous monitoring and surveillance of water quality.

During the 1950s and 1960s, problems on the Great Lakes came to a head. The parasitic sea lamprey had decimated fisheries as it invaded further into the waterway. In 1955 the

THE 1972 GREAT LAKES WATER QUALITY AGREEMENT

The Great Lakes Agreement established common water quality objectives to be achieved in both countries and three processes that would be carried out binationally. The first is control of pollution, which each country agreed to accomplish under its own laws. The chief objective was reduction of phosphorus levels to no more than l ppm (mg per litre) in discharges from large sewage treatment plants into lakes Erie and Ontario together with new limits on industry. Other objectives included elimination of oil, visible solid wastes and other nuisance conditions.

The second process was research on Great Lakes problems to be carried out separately in each country as well as cooperatively. Both countries established new Great Lakes research programs. Major cooperative research was carried out on pollution problems of the Upper Great Lakes and on pollution from land use and other sources.

The third process was surveillance and monitoring to identify problems and to measure progress in solving problems.

Research vessels collect water samples for the Great Lakes International Surveillance and Monitoring Program

Surveillance is carried out under a binational plan that is coordinated through the Great Lakes Regional Office of the IJC. The plan continues to change with evolution of new concepts of management. Initially, water chemistry was emphasized and levels of pollutants were reported. Now, the surveillance plan is designed to assess the health of the Great Lakes ecosystem and increasingly depends on monitoring effects of pollution on living organisms.

The agreement provided for a review of the objectives after five years and negotiation of a new agreement with different objectives if necessary. Tangible results had been achieved when the review was carried out in 1977. The total discharge of nutrients into the lakes had been noticeably reduced. Cultural, or man-made eutrophication, bacterial contamination and the more obvious nuisance conditions in rivers and nearshore waters had declined. However, new problems involving toxic chemicals had been revealed by research and the surveillance and monitoring program.

Public health warnings had been issued for consumption of certain species of fish in many locations. In the United States sale of certain fish was prohibited due to unsafe levels of PCBs and, later, mirex and other chemicals. In 1975, discovery of high levels of PCBs in lake trout on Isle Royale in Lake Superior demonstrated that the lakes were receiving toxic chemicals by long range atmospheric transport. These developments and the results of studies that were carried out after the 1972 agreement set the stage for the next major step in Great Lakes management.

The Upper Lakes study concluded that phosphorus objectives should be set for lakes Huron, Michigan and Superior. This development was significant because it recognized the Great Lakes as a single system and called for joint management objectives for Lake Michigan and its tributaries that had not previously been considered boundary waters.

The study on pollution from land use and other nonpoint sources was known as PLUARG (Pollution from Land Use Activities Reference Group). The study demonstrated that runoff from agriculture and urban areas was affecting water quality in the Great Lakes. This significant development confirmed that control of direct discharge of pollution from point sources alone into the Great Lakes and tributaries would not be enough to achieve the water quality objectives. It also called for control of nonpoint pollution into the Great Lakes from land runoff and the atmosphere.

The experience under the 1972 agreement demonstrated that, despite complex jurisdictional problems, binational joint management by Canada and the United States could protect the Great Lakes better than either country could alone. In 1978, a new Great Lakes Water Quality Agreement was signed that preserved the basic features of the first agreement and built on the previous results by setting up a new stage in joint management.

THE 1978 GREAT LAKES WATER QUALITY AGREEMENT

Like the 1972 agreement, the new agreement called for achieving common water quality objectives, improved pollution control throughout the basin, and continued monitoring by the IJC. As part of improved pollution control, the 1978 agreement called for setting target loadings for phosphorus for each lake and for virtual elimination of discharges of toxic chemicals. The target loadings were a step toward a new management goal that has come to be called "an ecosystem approach."

In contrast to the earlier agreement which called for protection of waters of the Great Lakes, the 1978 agreement calls for restoring and maintaining "the chemical, physical and biological integrity of the waters of the Great Lakes Basin Ecosystem." The ecosystem is defined as "...the interacting components of air, land and water and living organisms including man within the drainage basin of the St. Lawrence River."

In calling for target loadings for phosphorus, the 1978 agreement introduced the concept of mass balance into Great Lakes management. A target loading is the level that will not cause undesirable effects, including over-production of algae and anoxic conditions on lake bottoms. The mass balance approach calculates the amount of pollutant that remains active after all sources and losses are considered. All sources of phosphorus are considered in setting the controls that are needed to reach the target loading. Formerly phosphorus control was based on setting effluent limits to reduce pollution from direct discharges. Target loadings based on mass balance use mathematical models to determine levels of control that should protect the integrity of the ecosystem.

The mass balance concept is being applied to control of toxic substances into the Great Lakes, but understanding of the sources and effects of toxic chemicals in the lakes is not as complete. Although total elimination of toxic substances from the Great Lakes basin is the goal, the mass balance approach can be used to set priorities and direct pollution control efforts. Use of the mass balance concept for toxic substances is complicated by the large number of chemicals that have been found in fish, water or sediments. In order to set priorities for control, the Water Quality Board of the IJC has now divided them into groups with similar characteristics.

Another complication is the large number of diffuse sources such as land runoff, leaching from landfills, the atmosphere, and contaminated sediments. Still another complication is the difficulty of identifying effects of toxic chemicals. The levels of toxic chemicals in the Great Lakes are not high enough to cause immediately apparent health effects. However, damage occurs through long term exposure and bioaccumulation in the food chain. The extent of damage by synergism

Monitoring and research on the Great Lakes take place in all seasons.

AN ECOSYSTEM APPROACH TO MANAGEMENT

The adoption of an ecosystem approach to management is the result of growing understanding of the many interrelated and interdependent factors that govern the ecological health of the Great Lakes. An ecosystem approach does not depend on any one program or course of action. Rather it assumes a more comprehensive and interdisciplinary attitude that leads to wide interpretation of its practical meaning. Certain basic characteristics, however, mark the ecosystem approach.

First, it takes a broad, systemic view of the interaction among physical, chemical and biological components in the Great Lakes basin. The interdependence of the life in the lakes and the chemical/physical characteristics of the water is reflected in the use of biological indicators to monitor water quality and changes in the aquatic ecosystem. Examples include the use of herring gull eggs as an indicator of toxic pollutants, algal blooms as indicators of accelerated eutrophication and changes in species composition of aquatic communities as an indicator of habitat destruction. Biomonitoring for chronic toxicity can use zooplankton and phytoplankton to measure the effects of long term exposure to low levels of a toxic chemical on growth and reproduction.

Second, the ecosystem approach is geographically comprehensive, covering the entire system including land, air and water. New emphasis on the importance of atmospheric inputs of pollutants and the effects of land uses on water quality are evidence of the broad scope of management planning required in an ecosystem approach.

Finally, the ecosystem approach includes humans as a central factor in the wellbeing of the system. This suggests recognition of social, economic, technical and political variables that affect how humans use natural resources. Human culture, changing lifestyles and attitudes must be considered in an ecosystem approach because of their effects on the integrity of the ecosystem.

The ecosystem approach is a departure from an earlier focus on localized pollution, management of separate components of the ecosystem in isolation, and planning that neglects the profound influences of land uses on water quality. It is a framework for decision making that compels managers and planners to cooperate in devising integrated strategies of research and action to restore and protect the integrity of the Great Lakes ecosystem for the future. The evolution of management programs toward a full ecosystem approach is still in its early stages, but progress is being made.

or the cumulative result of exposure to many different chemicals is not known.

The 1978 agreement called for virtual zero discharge of persistent toxic chemicals because of severe and irreversible damage from bioconcentration of toxic substances present at very low levels in water. The effects include birth defects and reproductive failures in birds, and tumors in fish. A long term epidemiological study in Michigan has since shown that exposure to high concentrations of PCBs before birth and in breast milk affects the development of human infants. The elevated levels of PCBs in the mothers of these babies was due to consumption of certain fish from Lake Michigan.

Success in reducing phosphorus loadings under the Great Lakes agreement has provided a model to the world in binational resource management. The use of the mass balance approach for phosphorus set the stage for the much more difficult task of controlling toxic contamination. Further progress in cleaning up pollution from the past and preventing future degradation depends on fully applying an ecosystem approach to management.

CHAPTER SIX   THE FUTURE OF THE GREAT LAKES

Even though in earlier times the effects of pollution were often considered necessary results of prosperity and progress, the damage to human health and natural resources can no longer be ignored. Cooperation under the Great Lakes Water Quality Agreement and the national programs for environmental protection reflect the commitment of the people of the United States and Canada to prevent further degradation and protect the future of the Great Lakes.

Earlier chapters described the resources of the Great Lakes, how humans have used them and the physical, biological and chemical impacts of human activities. The previous chapter considered how a community of Great Lakes concern developed that included the public, scientists, and resource managers. Research in universities and government agencies has provided a substantial body of theory and information for practical management programs. The public, through participation as individual citizens and in organizations, have influenced elected officials.

Together, citizens and experts from both sides of the border provided the impetus for governments to cooperate and adopt more creative and effective management solutions to Great Lakes problems. The concept of an ecosystem approach to management evolved from experience in this broadly based Great Lakes community. But the story of the Great Lakes does not end here. Research continues, new methods of controlling and regulating impacts of human activities are being developed and the demand grows for rehabilitation and prevention of further damage.

While research continues to assist refinement of the mass balance and biomonitoring techniques, there is still an urgent need for better understanding of how toxic substances move through the Great Lakes ecosystem on land, in the air, and through aquatic foodchains. More information is needed about nonpoint sources such as land runoff, the atmosphere and groundwater, and about secondary pollution that may occur when substances combine chemically in air or water. As more is learned about the pathways of toxic chemicals, there is growing concern beyond the Great Lakes to the human food chain.

A broader scope of regulation of toxic chemicals may be necessary as research and monitoring reveals practices that are harmful. More stringent controls of waste disposal are already being applied in many locations. Agricultural practices are being examined because of the far-reaching effects of pesticides and fertilizers. Wetlands, forests, shorelines and other environmentally sensitive areas that are important to the Great Lakes ecosystem will have to be more strictly protected and, in some cases, rehabilitated and expanded.

For continued progress to be made in the protection of the Great Lakes, the people of the Great Lakes region must recognize their part in the ecosystem approach. We must control our technology and economic development so that we live within the ecosystem without injury to it. In return, the lakes and the lands surrounding them will continue to contribute to the quality of life for the people of the region and beyond.

GREAT LAKES CHARTER AND THE GREAT LAKES TOXIC SUBSTANCES CONTROL AGREEMENT

In 1985, the governors and premiers signed a Great Lakes Charter committing the states and provinces to regional cooperation in managing the Great Lakes. It was developed in response to interest in diverting water from the Great Lakes to other regions of the United States that face water shortages.

The charter assumes eventual agreement on a basin-wide management program based on principles that have already been accepted. Developing the charter was the first step toward a regional program for protecting the ecological integrity of the Great Lakes system. By signing the charter, the states and provinces also agreed to develop their own water management programs and to exchange information with each other before taking actions that affect the lakes.

The charter carries no legal enforcement authority in either country but depends on the voluntary good faith of the Great Lakes states and provinces. As a sign of regional unity against new exports of Great Lakes water, the charter probably makes federal support of diversion less likely in Ottawa and Washington.

In the spring of 1986, the governors of the eight Great Lakes states signed the Great Lakes Toxic Substances Control Agreement. This agreement pledges the states to co-operate in studying, managing and monitoring the lakes. The Agreement aims to reduce toxic substances to the maximum extent possible and to maintain environmental and public health priorities ahead of economic priorities. The premiers of the provinces of Ontario and Quebec support the agreement.

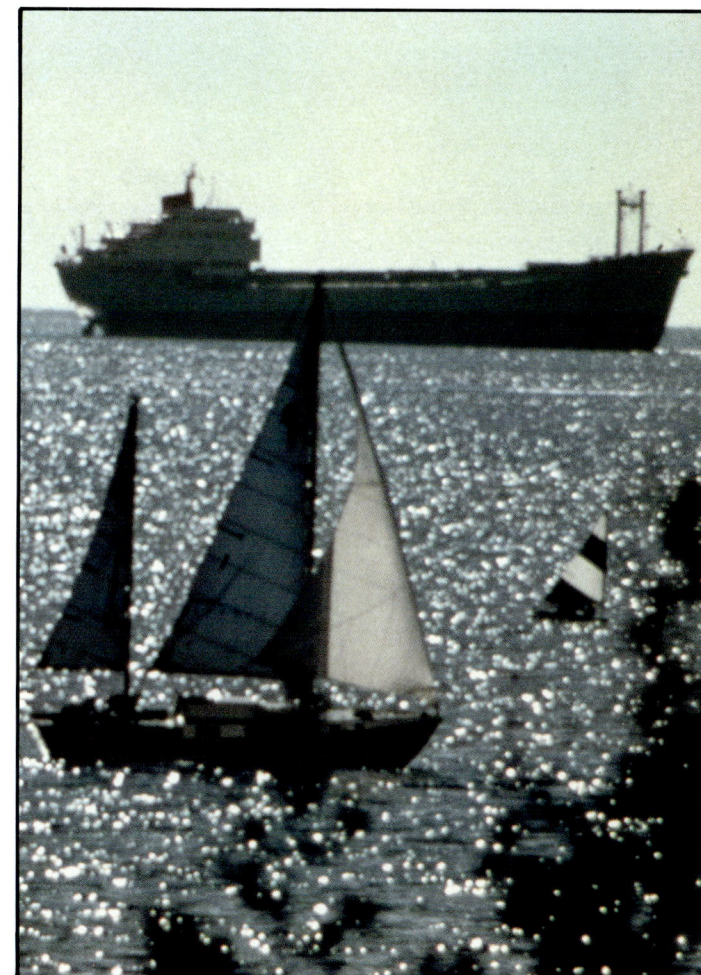

GLOSSARY

ALGA (ALGAE) - Simple one-celled or many-celled microorganisms capable of carrying on photosynthesis in aquatic ecosystems.

ANOXIA - The absence of oxygen necessary for sustaining most life. In aquatic ecosystems this refers to the absence of dissolved oxygen in water.

AREA OF CONCERN - An area recognized by the International Joint Commission where water uses are impaired or where objectives of the Great Lakes Water Quality Agreement or local environmental standards are not being achieved.

ATMOSPHERIC DEPOSITION - Pollution from the atmosphere associated with dry deposition in the form of dust, wet deposition in the form of rain and snow, or as a result of vapor exchanges.

BIOMAGNIFICATION - A cumulative increase in the concentration of a persistent substance in successively higher trophic levels of the foodchain.

BIOMASS - Total dry weight of all living organisms in a given area.

BIOMONITORING - The use of organisms to test the acute toxicity of substances in effluent discharges as well as the chronic toxicity of low-level pollutants in the ambient aquatic environment.

BIOCHEMICAL OXYGEN DEMAND - The amount of dissolved oxygen required for the bacterial decomposition of organic waste in water.

CARCINOGEN - Cancer-causing chemicals, substances or radiation.

CONSUMPTIVE USE - Permanent removal of water from a water body. Consumptive use may be due to evaporation or incorporation of water into a manufactured product.

DDT - Dichlorodiphenyltrichloroethane - a widely used, very persistent pesticide (now banned from production and use in many countries) in the chlorinated hydrocarbon group.

DISSOLVED OXYGEN - The amount of oxygen dissolved in water. See BIOCHEMICAL OXYGEN DEMAND.

DIVERSION - Transfer of water from one watershed to another.

DRAINAGE BASIN - A waterway and the land area drained by it.

ECOSYSTEM - The interacting complex of living organisms and their non-living environment.

EFFLUENT - Wastewaters discharged from industrial or municipal sewage treatment plants.

EPILIMNION - The warm, upper layer of water in a lake that occurs with summer stratification.

EROSION - The wearing away and transportation of soils, rocks and dissolved minerals from the land surface or along shorelines by rainfall, running water, or wave and current action.

EUTROPHICATION - The process of fertilization that causes high productivity and biomass in an aquatic ecosystem. Eutrophication can be a natural process or it can be a cultural process accelerated by an increase of nutrient loading to a lake by human activity.

EXOTIC SPECIES - Species that are not native to the Great Lakes and have been intentionally introduced or have inadvertently infiltrated the system.

FOODCHAIN - The process by which organisms in higher trophic levels gain energy by consuming organisms at lower trophic levels.

HYDROLOGIC CYCLE - The natural cycle of water on earth, including precipitation as rain and snow, runoff from land, storage in lakes, streams, and oceans, and evaporation and transpiration (from plants) into the atmosphere.

HYPOLIMNION - The cold, dense, lower layer of water in a lake that occurs with summer stratification.

LEACHATE - Materials suspended or dissolved in water and other liquids usually from waste sites that percolate through soils and rock layers.

MASS BALANCE - An approach to evaluating the sources, transport and fate of contaminants entering a water system as well as their effects on water quality. In a mass balance budget, the amounts of a contaminant entering the system less the quantity stored, transformed or degraded must equal the amount leaving the system. If inputs exceed outputs, pollutants are accumulating and contaminant levels are rising. Once a mass balance budget has been established for a pollutant of concern, the long-term effects on water quality can be simulated by mathematical modeling and priorities can be set for research and remedial action.

MESOTROPHIC - See TROPHIC STATUS

MONOCULTURE - Agriculture that is based on a single type of crop.

NONPOINT SOURCE - Source of pollution in which pollutants are discharged over a widespread area or from a number of small inputs rather than from distinct, identifiable sources.

NUTRIENT - A chemical that is an essential raw material for the growth and development of organisms.

OLIGOTROPHIC - See TROPHIC STATUS

PCBs - polychlorinated biphenyls - A class of persistent organic chemicals that bioaccumulate.

PATHOGEN - A disease-causing agent such as bacteria, viruses, and parasites.

PHOTOSYNTHESIS - A process occurring in the cells of green plants and some microorganisms in which solar energy is transformed into stored chemical energy.

PHYTOPLANKTON - Minute, microscopic aquatic vegetative life.

POINT SOURCE POLLUTION - A source of pollution that is distinct and identifiable, such as an outfall pipe from an industrial plant.

RESUSPENSION (of sediment) - The remixing of sediment particles and pollutants back into the water by storms, currents, organisms and human activities such as dredging.

SEICHE - An oscillation in water level from one end of a lake to another due to rapid changes in winds and atmospheric pressure. Most dramatic after an intense but local weather disturbance passes over one end of a large lake.

STRATIFICATION (or LAYERING) - The tendency in deep lakes for distinct layers of water to form as a result of vertical change in temperature and therefore in the density of water.

THERMOCLINE - A layer of water in deep lakes separating cool hypolimnion (lower layer) from the warm epilimnion (surface layer).

TOXIC SUBSTANCE - As defined in the Great Lakes Agreement, any substance that adversely affects the health or wellbeing of any living organism.

TROPHIC STATUS - A measure of the biological productivity in a body of water. Aquatic ecosystems are characterized as oligotrophic (low productivity), mesotrophic (medium productivity) or eutrophic (high productivity).

WIND SET-UP - A local rise in water levels caused by winds pushing water to one side of a lake.

ZOOPLANKTON - Minute aquatic animal life.

CONVERSION TABLE

Metric to Imperial Values
(approximate only)

1 metre =	3.28 feet
1 kilometre =	0.621 miles
1 kilogram =	2.2 pounds
1 square kilometre =	0.386 square miles
1 cubic kilometre =	0.24 cubic miles
1 liter =	0.264 U.S. gallons
1 cubic metre/second =	35.31 cubic feet/second
1 tonne =	1.1 short tons

REFERENCES AND SUGGESTIONS FOR FURTHER READING

AN AGREEMENT BETWEEN CANADA AND THE UNITED STATES OF AMERICA ON GREAT LAKES WATER QUALITY. April 15, 1972.

AN AGREEMENT BETWEEN CANADA AND THE UNITED STATES OF AMERICA ON GREAT LAKES WATER QUALITY. November 22, 1978.

Robert Allen. THE ILLUSTRATED NATURAL HISTORY OF CANADA: THE GREAT LAKES. Toronto: McClelland and Stewart, 1970.

ALTERNATIVES: PERSPECTIVES ON SOCIETY, TECHNOLOGY AND ENVIRONMENT. Special Issue. Saving the Great Lakes. Volume 13, No. 3, Septemebr/October, 1986.

William Ashworth. THE LATE, GREAT LAKES. New York: Knopf, 1986.

American Museum of Natural History. THE ENDURING GREAT LAKES. J. Rousmaniere, (ed). New York: W.W. Norton and Co. 1980.

D.B. Anderson. THE GREAT LAKES AS AN ENVIRONMENT. Toronto: University of Toronto Press, 1968.

Noel M. Burns. ERIE: THE LAKE THAT SURVIVED. Totowa, New Jersey: Rowman and Allanheld Publ., 1985.

Frank N. Egerton. OVERFISHING OR POLLUTION? CASE HISTORY OF A CONTROVERSY ON THE GREAT LAKES. Great Lakes Fishery Commission, Technical Report No. 41, Ann Arbor, Michigan, 1985.

Val Eichenlaub. WEATHER AND CLIMATE OF THE GREAT LAKES REGION. Notre Dame, Indiana, University of Notre Dame Press, 1979.

S.J. Eisenreich, C.J. Holland, T.C. Johnson. ATMOSPHERIC POLLUTANTS IN NATURAL WATER SYSTEMS. Ann Arbor, Mich.: Ann Arbor Science Publishers, 1980.

W.D. Ellis. LAND OF THE INLAND SEAS: THE HISTORIC AND BEAUTIFUL GREAT LAKES COUNTRY. Palo Alto: American West Publishing Co., 1974.

Lee Emery. REVIEW OF FISH SPECIES INTRODUCED INTO THE GREAT LAKES, 1819-1974. Great Lakes Fishery Commission, Technical Report No. 45, Ann Arbor, Michigan, 1985.

Environment Canada. A GUIDE TO THE GREAT LAKES WATER USE MAP. Policy Research and Social Analysis Division, Burlington, Ontario, 1978.

Environment Canada. GREAT LAKES CLIMATOLOGICAL ATLAS. A. Saulesleja (ed.) Atmospheric Environment Service. Canadian Government Publications Centre. (Cat. No. En56-70/1986): 1986.

Environment Canada and Ontario Ministry of the Environment. ST. CLAIR RIVER POLLUTION INVESTIGATION (SARNIA AREA). Unpublished Report under the Canada/Ontario Agreement Respecting Great Lakes Water Quality. Toronto, January, 1986.

Government of Canada. CURRENTS OF CHANGE; FINAL REPORT OF THE INQUIRY ON FEDERAL WATER POLICY. Ottawa, Canada, 1985.

Government of Canada, Ministry of State for Urban Affairs. THE GREAT LAKES MEGALOPOLIS. Ottawa, Canada, 1976.

Government of Quebec, St. Lawrence Development Secretariat. THE ST. LAWRENCE: A VITAL NATIONAL RESOURCE. Quebec, P.Q., 1985.

Great Lakes Basin Commission. GREAT LAKES BASIN COMMISSION FRAMEWORK STUDY. Public Information Office, Great Lakes Basin Commission, Ann Arbor, Michigan, 1976.

Great Lakes Commission. GREAT LAKES RESEARCH CHECKLIST. (Bibliography of Great Lakes Studies) 2200 Bonisteel Blvd, Ann Arbor, Michigan, semi-annually.

Great Lakes Fishery Commission. A JOINT STRATEGIC PLAN FOR MANAGEMENT OF THE GREAT LAKES FISHERIES. Ann Arbor, Michigan, 1980.

Great Lakes Fishery Commission. REHABILITATING GREAT LAKES ECOSYSTEMS. G.R. Francis, J.J. Magnuson, H.A. Regier, and D.R. Talhelm (eds). Technical Report No. 37, Ann Arbor, Michigan, 1979.

Great Lakes Tomorrow. DECISIONS FOR THE GREAT LAKES. Purdue University Calumet, Hammond, Indiana. 1982.

J.L. Hough. THE GEOLOGY OF THE GREAT LAKES. University of Illinois Press, 1958.

R.L. Heilmann, H.M. Mayer and E. Schenker. GREAT LAKES TRANSPORTATION IN THE EIGHTIES. University of Wisconsin Sea Grant Institute, Madison, Wisconsin, 1986.

International Association for Great Lakes Research. JOURNAL OF GREAT LAKES RESEARCH. Ann Arbor, Mich.: University of Michigan.

International Joint Commission. AN ENVIRONMENTAL MANAGEMENT STRATEGY FOR THE GREAT LAKES SYSTEM. Final Report, International Reference Group on Great Lakes Pollution from Land Use Activities (PLUARG). Windsor, Ontario. 1978.

International Joint Commission. 1985 REPORT ON GREAT LAKES WATER QUALITY. Report of the Great Lakes Water Quality Board. Presented at Kingston, Ontario, 1985.

International Joint Commission. LIMITED REGULATION OF LAKE ERIE. Washington, D.C. and Ottawa, Canada, 1983.

International Joint Commission. REPORTS ISSUED UNDER THE 1972 AND 1978 GREAT LAKES WATER QUALITY AGREEMENT; A BIBLIOGRAPHY. IJC Great Lakes Office, Windsor, 1983.

International Joint Commission. ANNOTATED BIBLIOGRAPHY OF PLUARG REPORTS. International reference Group on Great Lakes Pollution from Land Use Studies (PLUARG). Windsor, Ontario, 1979.

International Joint Commission. GREAT LAKES DIVERSIONS AND CONSUMPTIVE USES. Report by the International Great Lakes Diversion and Consumptive Uses Study Board, 1981.

Joseph L. Jacobsen. "PRENATAL EXPOSURE TO AN ENVIRONMENTAL TOXIN: A TEST OF MULTIPLE EFFECTS", DEVELOPMENTAL PSYCHOLOGY, Vol. 20, No. 4, 1984.

Michael Keating. TO THE LAST DROP: CANADA AND THE WORLD'S WATER CRISIS. Toronto: Macmillan of Canada: 1986.

Tom Kuchenberg. REFLECTIONS IN A TARNISHED MIRROR: THE USE AND ABUSE OF THE GREAT LAKES. Sturgeon Bay, Wisconsin: Golden Glow Publishing, 1978.

Jacques Le Strang (ed.). THE GREAT LAKES - ST. LAWRENCE SYSTEM. Boyne City, Michigan: Harbor House Publishers Seaway Review, 1985.

Marine Advisory Service of the Michigan Sea Grant College Program. LAKE SUPERIOR, MICHIGAN, HURON, ERIE, ONTARIO AND GREAT LAKES BASIN. Extension Bulletins E-1866 - 1871. Co-operative Extension Service, Michigan State University, East Lansing, Michigan, 1985.

P. McAvoy. THE GREAT LAKES CHARTER: TOWARD A BASIN-WIDE STRATEGY FOR MANAGING THE GREAT LAKES. Conference Proceedings, December 11-13, 1985, Cleveland, Ohio. Great Lakes Seminar: Diversions and Consumptive Use. Center for the Great Lakes, Chicago, Illinois.

Anne McCarthy. THE GREAT LAKES. New York: Crescent Books, 1985.

National Research Council of the United States and the Royal Society of Canada. THE GREAT LAKES WATER QUALITY AGREEMENT: AN EVOLVING INSTRUMENT FOR ECOSYSTEM MANAGEMENT. National Academy Press, Washington, D.C., 1985.

J.A. Nriagu and M.S. Simmons (eds). TOXIC CONTAMINANTS IN THE GREAT LAKES. New York: John Wiley and Sons, 1984.

C.W. Phillips and J.A.W. McCulloch. THE CLIMATE OF THE GREAT LAKES BASIN. Toronto, 1972.

Robert Spencer, John Kirton and Richard Nossal (eds). THE INTERNATIONAL JOINT COMMISSION SEVENTY YEARS ON. Centre for International Studies, University of Toronto, Toronto, Ont, 1981.

Walter Massey Tovell. THE GREAT LAKES. Toronto: Royal Ontario Museum, 1969.

TREATY BETWEEN THE UNITED STATES OF AMERICA AND GREAT BRITAIN RELATING TO BOUNDARY WATERS BETWEEN THE UNITED STATES AND CANADA. January 11, 1909.

U.S. Army Corps of Engineers. LAKE ERIE WASTE WATER MANAGEMENT STUDY. Summary Report. Buffalo District, Buffalo, New York, 1983.

U.S. Environmental Protection Agency. FIVE YEAR PROGRAM STRATEGY FOR GREAT LAKES NATIONAL PROGRAM OFFICE 1986 - 1990. Chicago, Illinois, 1985.

Wisconsin Coastal Management Council. THE INTERBASIN TRANSFER OF WATER: THE GREAT LAKES CONNECTION. Conference Proceedings, May 10 and 11, 1982. Milwaukee, Wisconsin. The Freshwater Society, Navaree, Minnesota 55392.

Wisconsin Sea Grant College Program. THE INVISIBLE MENACE: CONTAMINANTS IN THE GREAT LAKES. Madison, Wisconsin, 1980.

RELIEF, DRAINAGE AND URBAN AREAS (Page 2)

Canada, map, 1/5,000,000. Ottawa: Surveys and Mapping Branch, EMR, 1983.

Great Lakes Water Use, map, 1/1,584,000. Burlington: Inland Waters Directorate (Ontario Region), Environment Canada, 1980.

International Map of the World, map series, 1/1,000,000, sheets NL-17, NL-18, NM-15, NM-16. Ottawa: Surveys and Mapping Branch, EMR, various dates.

International Map of the World, map series, 1/1,000,000, sheets NK-16, NK-17, NK-18, NL-15, NL-16. Washington: USGS, Department of the Interior, various dates.

Karta Mira, map series, 1/2,500,000, sheets 31, 32, 47, 48. Budapest: National Office of Lands and Mapping, various dates.

United States, map, 1/2,500,000, east sheet. Washington: USGS, Department of the Interior, 1972.

GEOLOGY AND MINERAL RESOURCES (Page 6)

Douglas, R.J.W., Geology and Economic Minerals of Canada, Part B. Ottawa: Geological Survey of Canada, EMR, 1976.

Geologic Map of North America, 1/1,000,000. Washington: USGS, Department of the Interior, 1965.

Glacial Map of the United States East of the Rocky Mountains, 1/1,750,000. New York: Geological Society of America, 1959.

Hough, J.L., Geology of the Great Lakes. Urbana: University of Illinois Press, 1958.

International Reference Group on Great Lakes Pollution from Land Use Activities, Inventory of Land Use and Land Use Practices in the United States Great Lakes Basin, Vol. 1. Windsor: IJC, 1976.

National Atlas of Canada, 4th ed. Ottawa: Surveys and Mapping Branch, EMR, 1973.

National Atlas of Canada, 5th ed. Ottawa: Surveys and Mapping Branch, EMR, 1978 and later.

The National Atlas of the United States. Washington: USGS, Department of the Interior, 1970 and later.

Williams, H.R., Department of Geological Sciences, Brock University, St. Catharines, personal communication, 1986.

CLIMATE MAPS (Page 8)

Climatic Atlas Climatique - Canada, Map Series 1 - Temperature and Degree Days. Toronto: AES, Environment Canada, 1984.

Climatic Atlas of North and Central America, Vol. 1, Maps of Mean Temperature and Precipitation. Geneva: World Meteorological Organization, 1979.

Eichenlaub, Val L., Weather and Climate of the Great Lakes Basin. Notre Dame: University of Notre Dame Press, 1979.

Mudry, D., AES, Environment Canada, Ottawa, personal communication, 1986.

Phillips, D.W. and J.A.W. McCulloch, The Climate of the Great Lakes Basin, Climatological Studies No. 20. Toronto: AES, Environment Canada, 1972.

Shaw, A.B., Department of Geography, Brock University, personal communication, 1986.

Saulesleja, A. (ed.), Great Lakes Climatological Atlas. Toronto: AES, Environment Canada, 1986.

THE GREAT LAKES WATER SYSTEM (Page 10)

Great Lakes Diversion and Consumptive Uses. Windsor: IJC, 1985.

NFB Canada Map, no scale. Montreal: National Film Board of Canada, 1984.

HISTORICAL MAP (Page 16)

Transparency courtesy of National Map Collection, Public Archives of Canada, Ottawa.

LAND USE, FISHERIES AND EROSION (Page 19)

Coleman, D., Inland Waters and Lands Directorate, Environment Canada, Burlington, Ontario, personal communication, 1986.

Great Lakes Water Use, map, 1/1,584,000. Burlington: Inland Waters Directorate (Ontario Region), Environment Canada, 1980.

International Reference Group on Great Lakes Pollution from Land Use Activities, Inventory of Land Use and Land Use Practices in the Canadian Great Lakes Basin, Vol. 1. Windsor: IJC, 1977.

Ontario Commercial Fish Industry: Statistics on Landing, 1976-1980, updated to 1984. Toronto: Ontario Ministry of Natural Resources, ca. 1985.

Shore Use and Erosion Work Group, Great Lakes Basin Framework Study, Appendix 12, Shore Use and Erosion. Ann Arbor: Great Lakes Basin Commission, 1975.

Simpson-Lewis, W. et al., Canada's Special Resource Lands, Map Folio No. 4. Ottawa: Environment Canada, 1979.

WATERBORNE COMMERCE (Page 21)

Coastwise Shipping Statistics 1983. Ottawa: Statistics Canada, 1985.

International Seaborne Shipping Port Statistics 1983. Ottawa: Statistics Canada, 1985.

St. Lawrence Seaway Traffic Report for the 1983 Navigation Season. Ottawa: St. Lawrence Seaway Authority, ca. 1984.

Waterborne Commerce of the United States, Calendar Year 1983, Part 3 - Waterways and Harbors Great Lakes. Washington: Corps of Engineers, Department of the Army, ca. 1984.

RECREATION AND SPORTS (Page 23)

Amos, R., St. Catharines Blue Jays, St. Catharines, personal communication, 1986.

Annual Meeting of the Great Lakes Fishery Commission, Ann Arbor, 1986, Appendix XXXII.

Henley, G., School of Physical Education and Recreation, Brock University, St. Catharines, personal communication, 1986.

Dean, W.G. (ed.), Economic Atlas of Ontario. Toronto: University of Toronto Press, 1969.

Illinois, Indiana, Michigan, Minnesota, New York, Ohio, Pennsylvania, Wisconsin, road maps, various scales. Chicago: Rand McNally & Co., 1986.

Miscellaneous tourist pamphlets and brochures for Ontario and the states within the Great Lakes Basin.

Ontario, road map, 1/800,000 and 1/1,600,000. Toronto: Ontario Ministry of Transportation and Communications, 1986.

Shore Use and Erosion Work Group, Great Lakes Basin Framework Study, Appendix R9, Recreational Boating. Ann Arbor: Great Lakes Basin Commission, 1976.

Shore Use and Erosion Work Group, Great Lakes Basin Framework Study, Appendix 12, Shore Use and Erosion. Ann Arbor: Great Lakes Basin Commission, 1975.

The National Atlas of the United States. Washington: USGS, Department of the Interior, 1970 and later.

EMPLOYMENT AND INDUSTRIAL STRUCTURE (Page 25)

1980 Census of Population, Volume 1, Characteristics of the Population, Chap. C, General Social and Economic Characteristics, Parts 15, 16, 24, 25, 34, 37, 40 and 51. Washington: Bureau of the Census, US Department of Commerce, 1983.

1981 Census of Canada, Population etc., Selected Characteristics, Ontario. Ottawa: Statistics Canada, 1982.

1981 Census of Canada, Population, Economic Characteristcs, Ontario. Ottawa: Statistics Canada, 1984.

1981 Census of Canada. Reference Maps. Census Divisions and Subdivisions. Ottawa: Statistics Canada, 1982.

TRANSPORTATION AND ENERGY MAPS (Page 26)

Generating Station December Installed Capacity. Toronto: Ontario Hydro, 1985, mimeo.

Handy Railroad Atlas of the United States. Chicago: Rand McNally & Co., 1982.

Illinois, Indiana, Michigan, Minnesota, New York, Ohio, Pennsylvania, Wisconsin, road maps, various scales. Chicago: Rand McNally & Co., 1986.

Inventory of Power Plants in the United States 1985. Washington: Energy Information Administration, U.S. Department of Energy, 1986.

National Atlas of Canada, 5th ed. Ottawa: Surveys and Mapping Branch, EMR, 1978 and later.

Ontario, road map, 1/800,000 and 1/1,600,000. Toronto: Ontario Ministry of Transportation and Communications, 1986.

Sectional Aeronautical Charts, map series, 1/500,000, Chicago, Detroit, Green Bay and Lake Huron sheets. Washington: US Department of Commerce, 1986.

The Gifts of Nature. Toronto: Ontario Hydro, 1979.

The National Atlas of the United States. Washington: United States Geological Survey, Department of the Interior, 1970 and later.

VIA Rail pamphlets.

DISTRIBUTION OF POPULATION (Page 28)

1980 Census of Population, Vol. 1, Characteristics of the Population, Chap. C. General Social and Economic Characteristics, Parts 15, 16, 24, 25, 34, 37, 40 and 51. Washington: Bureau of the Census, U.S. Department of Commerce, 1983.

1981 Census of Canada, Population etc., Selected Characteristics, Ontario. Ottawa: Statistics Canada, 1982.

POLLUTION SOURCES AND TROPHIC STATUS (Page 34)

Beltram, R., U.S. EPA, Chicago, personal communication, 1986.

Great Lakes Water Quality Board, 1985 Report on Great Lakes Water Quality. Kingston: IJC, 1985.

Profiles of Environmental Quality, Region V, The Midwest. Chicago: U.S. EPA, 1979.

Report of the Niagara River Toxics Committee, 1984.

Saving the Great Lakes. Special issue of "Alternatives", Vol. 13, No. 3, 1986.

Toxics-Great Lakes-Hot Spots, map, no scale. Toronto: Pollution Probe, 1985.

Waste Site Inventories. Toronto: Waste Management Branch, Ontario MOE, 1986.

ECOREGIONS, DRAINAGE BASINS AND WETLANDS (Page 36)

Aquatic Ecoregions of USEPA Region V, draft map, 1/2,500,000, no date.

Ecodistricts of Southern Canada, draft maps, 1/2,000,000, no date.

International Reference Group on Great Lakes Pollution from Land Use Activities, Inventory of Land Use and Land Use Practices in the Canadian Great Lakes Basin, Vol. 1. Windsor: International Joint Commission 1977.

Rubec, C., Lands Directorate, Environment Canada, Ottawa, personal communication, 1986.

Shore Use and Erosion Work Group, Great Lakes Basin Framework Study, Appendix 10, Power. Ann Arbor: Great Lakes Basin Commission, 1975.

Wickware, G., Hunter and Associates, Mississauga, personal communication, 1987.

PHOTOGRAPHIC CREDITS

Pages 3, 7, 9, 11 (right) and 12: D. COWELL, Environment Canada

Pages 5, 29, 30 (center): Great Lakes Program Office, U.S. EPA, Chicago, Ill.

Pages 11 (center), 14, 20 (center), 22 (center), 38, 40 (left), 41: CCIW, Burlington, Ontario.

Pages 13 (center), 22 (right), 40 (right): U.S. National Parks Service, Indiana Dunes National Lakeshore.

Page 13 (right): University of Wisconsin, Extension Service.

Page 16: National Map Collection, Public Archives of Canada, Ottawa.

Page 17: Royal Ontario Museum.

Page 20 (right): F. BERKES.

Pages 24 (left), 30 (right): Lake Michigan Federation, Chicago, Ill.

Page 24 (center): Metropolitan Toronto Convention and Visitors Association.

Page 33: Ontario Ministry of the Environment.

Page 39: P. BERTRAM, Great Lakes National Program Office, U.S. EPA, Chicago, Ill.

PRODUCTION

Typesetting and photomechanical work for atlas maps by Commercial Photocopy Ltd., St. Catharines. Photomechanical work for folio map by Norman Wade Ltd., Toronto. Typesetting and layout of text by Kopy Kats Ltd., St. Catharines.

General assistance with the production of this atlas was given by Mr. H. BELZER, Printing Products Officer, Canadian Department of Supply and Services, Etobicoke, Ontario.